THE ALPHA WOMAN MEETS HER MATCH

THE ALPHA WOMAN MEETS HER MATCH

*How Today's Strong Women Can Find
Love and Happiness Without Settling*

Sonya Rhodes, PhD, and Susan Schneider

WILLIAM MORROW
An Imprint of HarperCollins*Publishers*

HarperCollins books may be purchased for educational, business, or sales promotional use. For information please e-mail the Special Markets Department at SPsales@harpercollins.com.

A hardcover edition of this book was published in 2014 by William Morrow, an imprint of HarperCollins Publishers.

FIRST WILLIAM MORROW PAPERBACK EDITION PUBLISHED 2015.

Designed by Lisa Stokes

Library of Congress Cataloging-in-Publication Data has been applied for.

ISBN 978-0-06-230984-6

15 16 17 18 19   ov/rrd   10 9 8 7 6 5 4 3 2 1

To Bob
—S.R.

To my daughter, India
—S.S.

CONTENTS

1 Loving Your Alpha   1

2 The Alpha/Beta Spectrum   13

3 Sex and the Alpha Woman   31

4 Bachelors, Boyfriends, and Married Men   47

5 The Alpha and Beta of Dating   73

6 Becoming a Couple   93

7 Affairs: Perfect Storms   123

8 Divorcing, Dating, Surviving, Thriving   143

9 Frequently Asked Questions   175

Afterword   185

References   189

Bibliography   193

Acknowledgments   195

THE ALPHA WOMAN MEETS HER MATCH

CHAPTER 1

LOVING YOUR ALPHA

IN THE YEARS I'VE spent building a thriving private practice as an individual and couples therapist, I've ridden the waves of the women's movement and the sexual revolution. But one day, as a client in her early thirties sat back with a sigh and said, "I guess I'm just your typical strong, overachieving woman with boy problems," I realized that I was seeing something distinctly new. Over the last decade or so, my practice has been crowded with women just like her: self-confident, accomplished, sexual—but unhappy and frustrated by their lack of success in relationships. These are the new Alpha women.

There's never been a better time to be an Alpha woman. She's on the rise in her education and in the professions. She's self-reliant, and she can explore her sexuality and make her own life choices. But many fear that marriage or a long-term relationship will somehow elude them.

In our society loud voices complain about women being too strong and too threatening and too sexual. The takeaway message? That women will overwhelm men with their strength and sexuality, and that no one will want to marry them. Let's lay that fear to rest: until the 1970s, well-educated, high-earning women were *less* likely to marry than less-educated women. But over the last four decades, marriage rates have either held constant or *increased* for the top 10 percent of female earners, according to a report from the Hamilton Project. Another study, cited by Stephanie Coontz in the *New York Times*, finds higher marriage rates for the top 15 percent of female earners. According to the Council on Contemporary Families: "College-educated women have a much greater likelihood of marrying at an older age than women of any other educational level. . . . College-educated women are more likely than any other group of women to report themselves happy in their marriage, whatever the level of their family income, and they are much less likely to think that financial security is the main benefit of marriage."

Until recently, women who married later than average had higher rates of divorce. Today, with every year a woman delays marriage, up to her early thirties, her chance of divorce decreases, and it does not rise again thereafter, reports Stephanie Coontz in the *New York Times*. For many of you reading this book, all of this is good news (*if* your plans include marriage!).

The dire predictions for women are way overinflated, and those who sound the alarms have their own agenda. Sometimes women themselves join the chorus of alarmists. A strong undercurrent of worry surfaces when they hear about a friend or colleague's divorce. One recently divorced woman told me that she could always count on these two questions: Had she worked too much? Was she a higher earner than her husband? These are women's secret fears. If a marriage breaks up, it has to be the woman's fault, right? And even our supposed allies may surprise us: that same woman who was interrogated by her friends was asked by a major women's magazine to write an essay about how her career ruined her marriage!

One woman in a focus group said, "I feel like an evolved person. I have a great career and great friends. I feel really strong in every part of my life except in relationships." I've heard many Alpha women express the fear that they won't find someone to love and to marry. Maybe they are too threatening to men, they say. Perhaps they should tone themselves down, they fret. I say, absolutely not. That is a big mistake.

Whenever I hear women say these things, I get angry—not at the women, of course, but at a culture that thrives on making dire predictions about the failed loves and lives of assertive, sexual Alpha women. It's simply ridiculous. For you, finding a mate is challenging, but the pool is large and your energy is strong.

What today's Alphas *can* do is be more careful about their choices. As it is, the women I treat are confident and overwhelmed, successful and self-doubting, sassy and diffident. They've been bruised by their experiences with men. The woman in the focus group added that she felt emotionally beaten up when a man she was seeing lost interest just as their relationship was on the verge of deepening. "I felt strong and good," she says. "I was ready to take the plunge. But after that I felt I couldn't trust my judgment anymore."

With egos shaken by unsuccessful relationships, women often feel uncharacteristically vulnerable and undone. When they walk into my office, they are seeking a mentor to guide them through the winding maze of dating, so that they can avoid the dead ends and arrive at the goal of finding someone with whom they can share their life. And I never encourage women to settle, tone themselves down, or blame themselves exclusively for problems in a relationship. None of these is an option. Never!

Images of those women paraded across my mind and their stories begged to be written about. Their dilemma is a telling part of today's zeitgeist. *The Alpha Woman Meets Her Match* is a boots-on-the-ground book that conveys everything I teach my patients and also includes the thoughts that I normally choose to keep to myself. The book is sourced from my clients' histories, focus groups, in-depth interviews, and from my deep layers of experience. You, the reader, will view clinical vignettes taken from my practice (composites of clients disguised to protect their identity). Every case study has a conclusion that you can apply to your own life. The stories will resonate with your experiences and offer plenty of insights and solutions for making the right choices in your personal life—without having to settle or compromise the person you are or wish to become.

TAKE BACK YOUR ALPHA

Ballbuster. Bitch. Bossy. Negativity swirls around assertive women. I know that the word *Alpha* paired with *woman* comes with a lot of baggage. At first I was advised to find a less controversial term than *Alpha woman*. But I decided to stick with it precisely *because* it has negative connotations. I do not think we should dumb down women's power and status by avoiding the Alpha in her. I think we should call it like it is. We're not doing a service, either to women or men, if we search for terms that don't ruffle feathers. The fact is there is a new gender-role reality, and it is retro to parse terms or, God forbid, threaten men's egos. I will never advise women to bend over backward to boost men's self-images by playing down their strengths. Those days are over.

Some fascinating research points to an urgent need for social norms to keep up with changing times. One study from the University of Chicago Booth School of Business found that when a woman earns the same or more than her mate, marital troubles often ensue. The wife may decide to work less or even go for a lower-paying job—a prime example of what it means to tone yourself down!—in order to protect the traditional belief that a man must be the family breadwinner. Even more amazing, the wife will often take on more of the household chores as a way to compensate for her greater earning power, with the aim of being nonthreatening to her husband. The academic term for this is *gender deviation neutralization*. Translation into English: if you dare to deviate from the norm (husband equals breadwinner), then you must somehow, in someway compensate for your abnormal behavior! This is a no-win situation; women should never tailor their behavior to meet social stereotypes. Ultimately, you'll hurt yourself *and* your relationship.

Over the last several decades, we've seen advances, like better birth-control options, exciting growth in economic opportunities for women, and the evolution of the feminist movement, as well as strong female role models in politics, the media, business, and academia. More women than men graduate from college and graduate school. Increasing numbers of women are enrolled in medical school. In 147 out of 150 of the biggest cities in the United States, unmarried, childless women under thirty earn 8 percent to 15 percent more than their male peers. Women contribute 40 percent of family wages, though they still make eighty cents to the man's dollar. In 25 percent of couples, women make more money than their husbands. In middle- and working-class families, women have more opportunities for economic and social mobility than men do. As you can see, neither the myth of the male breadwinner nor of the traditional female stands up to reality. We see the proof all around us: if women are successful in the business world and men are successful at home, both of which are clearly true, then the old stereotypes are just empty shells.

As a therapist, I see my clients' lives as microcosms of changes taking place in the larger society. Social and economic equality allows the expression of a wide range of gender-neutral personality and behavior for both men and women. Being competitive and dominant is not exclusively male any more than being nurturing and caring is exclusively female. Michael Kimmel, a sociologist who specializes in gender-role behavior, puts it this way: "Gender difference is the product of gender inequality, not the other way around."

Most striking to me is that as women have shaken off the constraints of old gender roles and become freer to pursue their sexuality and careers and personal fulfillment, new sets of problems have arisen. Everywhere I go—from the office to dinner parties—women of all ages relate to the Alpha identity and want relationship advice.

ALPHA WOMAN, BETA WOMAN

Today's Alpha woman is everywhere. In dress and style, the Alpha is the familiar, highly visible prototype; she wouldn't be caught dead in a 1980s power suit with padded shoulders that imitated male business attire. She is unabashedly sexy as well as career oriented. Her towering four-inch stilettos march off to the office, the store, the judge's chambers, and her lacquered-red soles send a "follow me" signal, straight to the bedroom.

She's the MD who manages a clinic like a well-oiled machine, or the self-confident Web editor who envisions herself running the company with her combination of tech skills and business savvy. She's the chic, assertive saleswoman who convinces you to buy an outfit you aren't sure you actually need. If she's young and feeling her way as an Alpha female, she may proudly sign her texts HBIC (head bitch in charge—an acronym I heard recently from a seventeen-year-old client of mine headed to the Ivy League, who could be the poster child for the new generation).

As I've studied and worked with women, I've discovered that our Beta sisters sometimes feel diminished or threatened by the Alpha prototype—but there is really no cause for this. I am not talking about good, bad, or better people; I am saying that all Alphas and Betas—in other words, all of us—are on a personality continuum, and most of us are a mix, with greater or lesser degrees of both.

Betas have less of a need for control, and they may have less interest in a leadership position than an Alpha would. In a group of women, the Alpha is the one who exerts power and influence through her ability to take charge of the conversation, while the Beta will tend to listen and support. In the extremes of both, an Alpha may be too confrontational; a Beta may be too passive. Fortunately, people are malleable, and you can modify some of your behavior for a better balance.

Can you be an Alpha if you're not a big earner or powerful out in the working world? Of course! Lily, a physician and a mother of two, works between fifteen and twenty hours a week to her husband's seventy hours plus. She puts it this way: "I'm an Alpha in disguise. I don't wear my Alpha on my sleeve."

Like Lily, many strong Betas carve out a niche for themselves within a relationship; they may control the finances or decisions about the children, for example. "I'm a little afraid of direct confrontation," Lily says. "I will tend to avoid it. I look like I'm easygoing and amenable and I don't always show my forceful side, but I do like to get my way." Alpha? Beta? It isn't always either/or, and Alpha is not better than Beta. Far more important is the degree of each that you have in your personality, and I will show you how that works in chapter 2, where you'll plot your profile on the Alpha/Beta spectrum. You may be a Beta, with anywhere from a handful to a big helping of Alpha, or an Alpha with strong to middling Beta tendencies, or an extreme Alpha, with practically no Beta at all. You may be pretty much a hybrid, with equal amounts of both. I'm betting that you've got some Alpha no matter who you are.

Funny, strong, independent, and comfortable in her own skin, the Alpha believes in herself—but has some blind spots. She assumes that as an Alpha female she should be partnered with an Alpha male.

But clinical experience has shown me that this partnership is at the greatest risk for divorce, because two Alphas will tend to compete for power and dominance. I will show Alpha women how they can learn to envision and accept themselves as the Alpha in a relationship with a Beta man, who might just make the best fit.

THE NEW "CATCH"

The Beta man is out there in the culture, in the media, and in the sociologists' studies and statistics—and he's a great catch. He might be that dad pushing a stroller down the street, or the dad who is the Pied Piper of the playground set, or the father who knows the politics of the kids' PTA far better than his working wife does. A *New Yorker* magazine cartoon features two Old West–style gunslinger hombres with their infants in BabyBjörns standing in a bar negotiating for a play date. A new ad campaign for shaving cream suggests men "man up," a playful poke both at traditional notions of manhood and at today's softer guy.

Today's Beta guy is transformed and more complicated than the sensitive guy from the eighties and nineties. *Real Men Don't Eat Quiche,* a bestselling book in the eighties, satirized the sensitive man who was trying very, very hard to be acceptable to feminists. We've come further by now! The Beta man is no longer the guy assumed to be gay if he likes yoga, dresses well, or is a vegan. His ego doesn't depend on scoring macho points. He is dependable, responsible, and supportive.

Many Alpha women have a sexual Achilles' heel: openly sexual as they are, they still expect the man to take the lead in bed, which gets in the way of their falling for the tender lover, the Beta male. I call it the *Fifty Shades of Grey* syndrome, based on the series that found such a willing audience among Alpha dynamos who feel some sneaky retro shame about their sexual appetites. An Alpha who is secretly embarrassed by her intense sexual fantasies may feign passivity in order for the man to take the lead, so she can be taken. Her shame, which is not obvious to her, is paradoxical, contradicting everything about this alluring, sexy, spunky woman.

I will show how Beta males are—or can be—the best lovers because they want *you* to get off, too. With men, we tend to categorize Alphas as sexy, Betas as weak. Forget that! I will show you how to stop compartmentalizing and find the more complex man you're really looking for.

But what do women and men really feel about the nonmacho male? After I'd begun thinking about Alpha female–Beta male partnerships, I mentioned to an Alpha friend of mine that her husband was a great Beta guy. Although I meant it as a compliment—her husband is a nurturing family man and a supercreative graphic designer who works on a vintage letterpress machine in his studio—I could tell from her body language that she was a little insulted. It made me realize just how loaded these terms are.

The old hierarchy of Alpha and Beta, in which the highest-ranking Alpha males run the show, isn't operative anymore. Not every man is an Alpha player nor an Omega loser desultorily plucking his guitar on an old futon in his mom's basement. Alpha players are alive and well—and enabled by technology (their best friend!)—and so are hopeless wimps and slackers. But most of the men I see—hailing everywhere from Wall Street to the suburbs—*do* seek equal, balanced relationships: a 2010 Pew poll found that 62 percent of both men and women believe that the best marriage depends on a true partnership—in other words, that ever-desirable, ever-elusive state of nirvana we call equality. Of course, making that a reality is still a huge challenge in spite of all the changes.

Alpha women like to lead, and Beta guys do not mind following.

But am I advocating inequality? A good Alpha woman–Beta man partnership can benefit both partners if they respect each other. If the Beta guy knows how and when to push back, the power balance can skew in the direction of the Alpha woman without harm being done to the relationship. When I see successful marriages like a rabbi wife wedded to a stay-at-home dad who happily watches the couple's four children, an attorney wife whose bike-mad husband runs a suburban bicycle shop, or the male elementary-school teacher married to the female physician, I'm heartened. These couples have found their bliss.

A MODERN VISION OF LIFE

I do not believe that the start of the era of the Alpha woman means the end of men. The new era isn't about women being up and men being down. Alpha isn't better; nor is Beta. The Alphas and the Betas of the world can balance each other out, smooth the rough edges. Alphas need some Beta and Betas need some Alpha to make them well rounded and equipped to succeed in the twenty-first century. You will see how this works in relationships.

I will help you know who you are and find a relationship that's the best fit. I will explain a great therapist's tool—the concept of positive complementarity, which is the way couples balance and complement each other's strengths and weaknesses—in order to build a relationship with a strong, sustainable structure. I will discuss how sharing a vision of life, which involves the concept of partnering, is probably *the* greatest predictor of a successful marriage. The new gender roles require new paradigms for understanding the politics and dynamics of relationships. As gender roles have become fluid, previously rock-solid characteristics for men and women have liquefied. This is totally for the good of all.

These are confusing times. The Alpha woman–Beta man partnership goes against cultural traditions that we've all been taught. And so much else is going against tradition that sociologists' and psychologists' heads are spinning: the unique-to-our-times decision of many women to marry later or not to marry at all; prolonged bachelorhood; and single motherhood, either by choice or by divorce. It's quite a challenge!

GETTING TO "AHA"

Unsurprisingly, when a client comes to my office for the first time, she is distressed over a bad breakup or by a relationship that just won't take. She is feeling battered and frustrated by her experiences with men, and she is on the cusp of desperation. I spend our initial sessions getting to know her intimately. I encourage her to share the narrative of her life: her successes and disappointments, her longings and desires, her vision of her future, her values, and her choices and behavior in relationships. I get a clear picture of the man or men she dates and how she goes about her dating life. Because I conceive of therapy as an interactive partnership, we work together to identify patterns in her love life. By the third or fourth session, I usually have an idea of what is getting in the way of her being more successful in the dating world.

Since my clients are usually quite empowered in most arenas of their lives, I focus on what prevents them from experiencing the same kind of fulfillment in relationships. I never shy away from being a client's advocate, guide, and confidante. I am very direct, but always in a caring context.

I have suffered along with many gutsy women clients as they face the deeply personal challenges that go into making an eleventh-hour decision about single motherhood. I will advise younger women on how to avoid getting backed into a corner—that is, how to know when to give up on the good-time guy and start focusing on someone who wants what you want. Some Alpha women who start seeking a serious relationship in their thirties may find that men their own age resist being pressured into making a commitment and will opt to date younger women. If you're at that place, I will walk you through your options as well as how to reinvent yourself with an eye toward a great future. (Trust me. You can definitely do it.)

In my comfortable office, men and women have the rare chance to look into their hearts. I will show just how much, for better or for worse, online dating and tech devices have revolutionized every aspect of the age-old search for sex, love, and meaningful relationships. I will come down squarely in the position of yes, it's convenient and helpful, but no, you are not just an algorithm.

I spend my days happily analyzing relationship patterns and helping people reexamine their expectations and rebalance their most intimate connections. It's an ongoing drama in which men and women are now trading the leading roles. Every strong, independent woman I work with wants a connection with a flexible, adaptable partner—someone who will love, value, and respect her. I stay with her as she rides the wild dating roller coaster and help her put on the brakes in the right place. I work with men who are struggling with a new economic reality and definitions of manhood. As I share the fascinating and highly relatable stories that I hear from my clients, I am dead certain that you will experience one aha moment after another.

My office provides a wide-open window into the future of relationships in our society. The view from here—complicated, challenging, and exciting—gives me reason to think that men and women, whose ideals include equality based on new definitions of gender roles, can work toward and practice their ideals. It makes me optimistic about the future. I want to share my optimism and expertise with you, Alpha and Beta, single and married or divorced, with children or not.

CHAPTER 2

THE ALPHA/BETA SPECTRUM

HERE'S A RADICAL THOUGHT: Suppose, just suppose, that most of the personality characteristics associated with males and females are culturally determined, and further suppose that all the endless discussions you've heard about the vast differences between the sexes and the resulting communication gap, are exaggerated. Assume for a moment that men and women are more *alike* than different.

While I am not suggesting the end of gender, there is strong evidence from research in sociology and neurobiology that culturally acceptable male and female behavior is more about social norms than biology. In my own psychoanalytic training, I was taught that because men's sexual organs were outside their bodies and women's were inside, men were innately more aggressive and women more passive. Even as a young, untutored therapist this sounded like BS. What about breasts? They stuck right out there on a woman's chest. How did the theory of female passivity account for that, Dr. Freud?

In 2005, Janet Hyde, PhD, published a famous meta-analytic review of research on gender and sexuality called the Gender Similarities Hypothesis. Dr. Hyde, a psychologist at the University of Wisconsin–Madison, tested the gender differences model, which maintains that women and men are profoundly different, biologically and psychologically, by examining two decades' worth of gender studies, forty-six in all. Her findings? A person's gender had *little or no* impact on most psychological traits, including aggression and passivity.

Dr. Hyde went on to point out that men and women have been taught they come from "different planets," and therefore speak different languages. Unfortunately, she says, these ideas are so widely disseminated that they become self-fulfilling: Men learn that they're poor communicators and inept with emotions, so they clam up and thus prove it. Women are taught they aren't destined for leadership, so they put the brakes on at a safe distance and settle for something more in keeping with their "natural" talents (like nurturing). When you consider the huge toll these beliefs have taken on the personal and professional lives of both women and men, you just might feel that it's time for a change. I do.

In the 1950s and 1960s, an Alpha male paired with a Beta female was *the* couple. They complemented each other: he, the dominant breadwinner; she, the deferential stay-at-home wife and mother, embodied by June Cleaver and other idealized 1950s housewives. In an upwardly mobile postwar economy, these gender roles provided stability for the nuclear family. It made sense in terms of each partner having a clearly defined role. But those culturally defined norms for women became so distorted—so extreme—that women, fueled by the sixties counterculture, rebelled against the narrow definition of femininity, and the women's movement gathered momentum.

But the Alpha male is still mythologized as the most virile and desirable male, and Beta males are still getting a lackluster score on the manhood scale. Alpha women have been caricatured as pushy, bitchy, and unfeminine, while the old-fashioned submissive Beta woman conjures a powerful nostalgia. Even after their expiration date, these unfortunate stereotypes have had an amazing shelf life. As long as we still buy them, we perpetuate distorted views of ourselves that lead to making unhealthy romantic choices.

I propose that we look at personality characteristics on an Alpha/Beta spectrum that applies to both genders. This way we can see ourselves as individuals, not aggregates of culturally determined male and female characteristics. The terms are used nonjudgmentally, to give people the tools to evaluate themselves and their relationships. Every woman and man lands at some unique, nuanced point on the spectrum; no one is one-dimensional. Defining your profile on the Alpha/Beta spectrum is a matter of learning and owning all your qualities: strengths and weaknesses alike.

On the spectrum, you'll find the extremes of Alphas and Betas bookending many degrees and combinations of characteristics in between. Some people are clearly at the extremes, while others will find themselves tilting more in one direction than the other. Still others are hybrids with fairly equal helpings of both types. If you're dealing with difficult relationship issues in the twenty-first century (and who isn't?), using this spectrum will help you to understand and adapt to the massive cultural shifts in gender roles and identities and to expand your choices and build better relationships.

TEASING OUT THE TERMS

Are you adventurous, career oriented, and self-assured? Do you savor the idea of yourself as an Alpha? Some of the women who come to my office refer to themselves matter-of-factly as Alpha, though each of these women is, in my view, quite different. In fact, there is no single, catchall Alpha profile. I divide Alphas into high, middle, and low, with a high Alpha, for example, being unambiguously independent, unafraid of confrontation, assertive, decisive, and somewhat bossy. She is usually at the center of the action socially, a leader and a connecter, who brings people together and organizes shared activities. High Alphas are *very* determined: they go after what they want and generally get it.

Betas also come in high, middle, and low, and, depending on where you score on the Beta scale, you are nurturing, tuned-in emotionally, and collaborative. In a group, Betas don't mind playing a supportive rather than a leading role. They are self-reliant but do not have a powerful need to be the boss. Today's Beta woman is not the Beta woman of the past. She is in touch with her inner Alpha; she may exert her Alpha more at home than at work, or vice versa. People with high amounts of Beta will tend to avoid confrontation, but if they also have a good sprinkling of Alpha, they *will* stand up for what they believe. With an Alpha man who likes to dominate, a Beta female's ability to accommodate can create a good balance, but I have noticed that more and more Beta women are falling for Beta guys who will be a strong partner, share in work and child care, and have the potential to be a best friend.

The new Beta male is more complicated and desirable than the sensitive guy of the 1980s and 1990s. He is emotionally accessible and cooperative. Describing her Beta boyfriend, a twenty-eight-year-old woman said, "We're equals. He says he's trainable; just tell him what I need and he'll do it. He has a strong mom, so he's respectful. He's solid in his Betaness. I can be the leader and it's OK with me and with him."

Above all, a solid Beta has the ego strength not to be afraid of strong women. Although taking on a battle may not be his first inclination, the Beta male will push back when necessary. He's no wuss: he is cooperative but not compliant, accomplished but not a workaholic, assertive but not confrontational. He is the man many contemporary women have been waiting for, but he is not adequately appreciated in a culture where the Alpha male has reigned supreme.

THE PERSONALITY PROFILES

Here, a breakdown of the two types that includes strengths and weaknesses:

Alpha

- **Positive:** independent; self-assured; assertive; adventurous; ambitious; risk taker; determined; high energy; leader.

- **Negative:** overconfident; controlling; stubborn; tends to be critical but doesn't take criticism well; hierarchical; tends to cover insecurities with bravado; finds it difficult to tolerate feelings of helplessness or vulnerability; must be the king or queen bee.

- **Positive/negative:** intense; confrontational (might go for the jugular too often, but has the guts to face conflict); can communicate directly, but sometimes is too blunt.

Beta

- **Positive:** emotionally available; collaborative; mellow; reliable; compassionate; caring lover; relationship oriented; aspires to be a good partner; a team player; a good confidante; responsible.

- **Negative:** difficulty expressing anger; overly anxious; too self-critical; passive-aggressive; sometimes too laid-back; may relinquish power when it is not in his/her best interest; may communicate so indirectly that she/he obscures the message; overly concerned with what people think.

- **Positive/negative:** accommodating (will bend over backward too often, but can cooperate for mutual benefit); wants to please but sometimes at his/her own expense; not competitive (on the downside, may give in too quickly; on the upside, can allow someone else to take the spotlight); avoids power struggles but may be bullied.

THE ALPHA/BETA PERSONALITY QUESTIONNAIRE

I developed this questionnaire over the course of many months to identify personality traits and relationship styles. Go through the statements below, and check the ones that apply to you. Don't over-think. And remember: there are no right or wrong answers. I have found this tool incredibly helpful for people seeking a deeper under-standing of themselves and their choices, for those looking for a part-ner who's their best match, and for evaluating the issues and conflicts in an already-existing relationship.

At the end of the questionnaire, you will find a key telling you how to tally your score. Once you determine your personal level of Alpha and Beta, you can plot your personality type on the graph that follows.

1. I tend to be bossy.
2. I try hard to please my partner.
3. I'm hot-tempered.
4. I put friendships above ambition.
5. People sometimes say I'm arrogant.
6. I try to see other points of view.
7. I was/am a big party person in college.
8. I tend to dwell on my mistakes.

9. I love the adrenaline rush of gambling.

10. I procrastinate on projects at home and at work.

11. I don't really keep to any budget.

12. I tend to be cautious about spending money.

13. I can crush people with my criticism.

14. I empathize easily with other people's problems.

15. I'm a doer, not a talker.

16. I'm cautious about most decisions.

17. I am superconfident.

18. I frequently stay awake at night thinking about what I should have said.

19. I don't hesitate to assert my needs in a relationship.

20. I shut down when I am overwhelmed.

21. I'm gutsier than a lot of my friends.

22. I love playing with kids.

23. Once I make up my mind, I'm hard to budge.

24. I hate confrontations.

25. I am sometimes so confident that I underestimate the competition.

26. I will do almost anything to avoid a fight with a friend.

27. I'm a control freak; if I don't do it, it doesn't get done.

28. I go out of my way to make people feel comfortable.

29. I frequently cancel dates at the last minute.

30. I love a tête-à-tête with a close friend more than a party.

31. I'm happy in the spotlight.

32. I need the affirmation of others to feel really good about myself.

33. I like to get my way.

34. I am hesitant to take credit for work I do as part of a team.

35. I act confident even if I am not feeling it.

36. I am good at taking care of other people.

37. I have an entrepreneurial spirit.

38. When I'm dating, I feel insecure about whether men will find me attractive.

39. I always speak my mind.

40. I'm cautious with people I don't know.

41. Other people's achievements make me work harder.

42. I try to intuit other people's feelings.

43. I am very competitive.

44. It's better to be gentle than blunt.

45. I don't like apologizing.

46. I find myself apologizing for many things that happen.

47. I am very intense about my life and keep my goals front and center.

48. I worry about other people's opinions of me.

49. Other people make more mistakes than I do.

50. I tend to be a very laid-back person.

51. I am aggressive about getting what I want.

52. I take pride in being a caring lover.

53. I am smarter than most people.

54. I often become overwhelmed when I am angry.

55. I do most things to the max.

56. I worry about my partner cheating on me.

57. I love exploring new places and meeting new people.

58. For men: I would never talk down to a woman.

59. Taking risks is really fun.

60. I'm a little inhibited sexually.

61. I naturally take the lead in groups.

62. It's important to be a good partner in a relationship.

63. For women: I am never intimidated by men.

64. I'm a worrier.

65. People kid me about how I take up all the space in a room.

66. I let people know I'm angry without actually saying so.

67. I love being challenged.

68. A perfect evening is to order in and watch a movie.

69. Other people come up short a lot of the time.

70. I am devastated if I unintentionally hurt someone's feelings.

71. I like to take on a difficult project and prove I can do it.

72. I hate dealing with money problems.

73. I am a dominant person.

74. I have benefited from some therapy.

75. Sometimes it is hard not to make a snarky comment.

76. I feel guilty a lot.

77. Having power is a turn-on.

78. I almost always see an argument from both sides.

79. I like to experiment sexually.

80. I'm a team player.

81. I make sure that people pay attention to me.

82. Ouch! Sometimes people can really hurt me.

83. My arguments are usually hard-hitting.

84. When things go wrong, I usually blame myself.

85. I know just when to go in for the kill.

86. I follow the rules.

87. I don't really care what people think of me.

88. I respect the opinions of others.

89. My opinions are hard-and-fast.

90. I sometimes have to talk myself out of self-doubt.

91. I take the sexual initiative.

92. It's important to strive for consensus.

93. I initiate in many ways: choosing a restaurant, a movie, an apartment, etc.

94. I am a good mediator, because I don't take sides.

95. I make decisions quickly; why waste time?

96. I try to please people a lot.

97. I like to give advice.
98. I tend to be anxious in new situations.
99. If it's important, I'll play hardball in a negotiation.
100. I hate to upset other people.

To get your score, count up and total the **even** numbers that you checked. Multiply by 2 and add a percent sign to your score. This is your Beta score. Do the same for the **odd** numbers that you checked. This is your Alpha score. Example: if you checked twenty **even** numbers and thirty **odd** numbers, you would be 40 percent Beta and 60 percent Alpha. On the graph below, you will plot the coordinates of your two scores by placing your Beta percentage along the bottom of the graph and your Alpha along the vertical. In which box do the lines intersect? Are you higher in Alpha or Beta? By a lot or a little? If your percentages are close—within 1 to 10 percentage points—you are a hybrid (almost equal in both).

If you have a partner, ask him/her to do the questionnaire. Score it the same way you did for yourself. Now plot him/her on the graph. Are you two in the same box or in different ones? After the graph, take a look at the nine personality profiles that match up with the graph's boxes. The profiles are designed to elucidate the potential of various relationship matches, which would be either positive and comfortable, challenging and conflicted, or downright hazardous for you.

ALPHA / BETA GRAPH

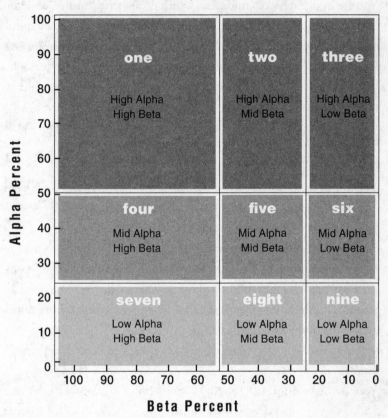

One

You are a true hybrid: high in Alpha and Beta. You are very self-confident and ambitious, and you will lead as well as compromise in a relationship. This is an unusual profile since most of us are not high in both qualities. You will match with many people, but be careful about a partner who is in the nine box; that relationship will be codependent since you will do all the work. Your ideal match is with someone similar to yourself (one, four, two, five).

Two

You are high Alpha and mid Beta, which means that you are dominant in most relationships but have the capacity to collaborate and compromise. However, you have to guard against imposing your strong will and overpowering people. You will match up well with a partner who has a strong mid-to-high Beta profile and will allow your Alpha to lead. Your best match is with someone more laid-back than you, who will help you take the edge off when necessary (four or seven).

Three

You are exceedingly dominant, in fact, downright bossy. Since your controlling Alpha is so strong, you need to soften it by developing your Beta side and allowing yourself to feel vulnerable. Your best fit is a partner with high Beta qualities—but he or she should also have at least a middle dose of Alpha, or else you will roll over him/her. Look for a partner who falls in four or five. If your partner is too much like you (high Alpha/low Beta), the two of you will end up in endless arguments and power struggles.

Four

You are a good mixture of Alpha and Beta; you probably get along with everyone and are well liked. You are confident without being overbearing. As a cooperative person, you may prefer letting your partner take the lead—but you are not a pushover. You will partner well with a strong Alpha (one, two), since you can hold your own. However, you will be comfortable in a stable, secure relationship with another person like yourself (four).

Five

You are a hybrid of mid Alpha and mid Beta. You are easygoing, and with your good relationship skills, you can create an equal, compatible relationship with someone like yourself (five). Since both of you tend to shy away from confrontation, this safe, secure partnership would have only a low degree of conflict. However, because you are a hybrid, you have several more challenging options (one, two, three). With any of these matches, you would be the nurturer and your partner would be the leader. You might have to develop a little more Alpha so that you can occasionally push back.

Six

You are confident in many situations, but you are not intuitive about the feelings of others and tend not to work hard to maintain your relationships. You are super low-key, sometimes too laid-back, and conflict avoidant. You need a partner who is higher in Beta than you are (two, five), so that you can learn to be more tuned-in to others.

Seven

You are very accommodating and sensitive, and you seek security and stability in your relationships. You do not like to rock the boat and tend to avoid competition and confrontation. Your strength is in your emotional accessibility; you seek deep relationships and are able to compromise, but you lack spunk and confidence. Your most complementary partnerships are with the stronger Alphas—but beware of becoming codependent with someone who dominates you.

Eight

As an emotional person you value your relationships a lot, but you lack self-confidence and find it difficult to sound your own horn. Although you have strong opinions, you are uncomfortable fighting for what you believe in. You might be drawn to partners with high Alpha (two or three), which puts you at risk of being bullied. Because you do not like confrontations and seek compatibility, you need to learn not to back away from challenges. You would do best with a partner similar to you (seven or eight) or a mid Alpha (four or five).

Nine

You are unsure of yourself and too conforming. Passive, anxious, and excessively self-critical, you are sometimes afraid of your own shadow and worry way too much about what people think. You tend to misjudge others' motives and intentions. Before you get into a relationship, take stock and think about how to develop more self-confidence. Otherwise, you will be taken advantage of and possibly even mistreated. Be careful. You are vulnerable!

IT'S A MATCH

This is how I evaluated four single women of different ages, backgrounds, and occupations who took the questionnaire.

Carson, 21

With a score of 33 percent Alpha and 38 percent Beta, Carson is mid Alpha/mid Beta (five). A senior at an all-women's college in Georgia, Carson wants to go to graduate school in Middle East studies and eventually work overseas for the government. She believes she can do anything she sets her mind to and she knows her own mind. From a religious Southern family, she adheres to certain standards for herself, but does not judge other people. She doesn't believe in having sex before marriage, and getting married is a goal that's way at the bottom of her to-do list. "All my friends hook up," she says. "I don't, but I understand why they do. If I weren't religious, I'd do it, too." She emphatically does not want a relationship, because "I want to discover my own path before I involve someone else." Carson had a boyfriend in her sophomore year, but says, "He didn't understand why I was so career driven. He didn't respect the goals I have for myself. He was wife hunting, and I said, 'See you later!'" Someday, she says, she'll probably get married, but for now she wants to study and work. She names Hillary Clinton as her role model. Her number-one goal is to live in the Middle East and serve others. "It's so important," she says, "to share encouragement, optimism, and love." When she's ready, Carson's best matchup will fall into the one, two, or three boxes (and he should be prepared to travel!).

Sophie, 26

At 70 percent Alpha and 30 percent Beta, Sophie is high Alpha/mid Beta (two). She is bossy, hot-tempered, outspoken, suffers fools badly, and unintimidated by men. At the same time friends are very important to her, she hates to upset people, and she does not put her ambitions above her friendships. She is uneasy with her habit of getting too quickly involved with someone who interests her—and then ending it when the guy wants to push the relationship further and she begins to feel hemmed in. Men invariably feel led on and rejected. She has too much work to do, too many degrees to achieve, and too many places to go. She likes the feeling of having power, but she doesn't like the fact that she hurts people. As a high Alpha, Sophie moves too fast; she is on a roller coaster of excitement and disappointment. If she slows down, she'll feel more in control and less guilty. When she is ready to look for a serious relationship, her good prospects will fall into the four or seven boxes: Sophie's best partner will be a man who lets her take the lead but knows how to push back; she will do well with someone steady who can help her off the roller coaster but who can meet her on a solid intellectual and emotional footing.

Suzie, 29

Her score is 48 percent Alpha and 76 percent Beta. Suzie has just finished her residency as a physician at a large metropolitan hospital and is focused on finding a partner. At her Ivy League college and at medical school she explored relationships with many different kinds of men: the athlete, the charmer, the dreamer, and the dutiful. In between these relationships, she enjoyed casual sex with a number of peers. Through these experiences, Suzie learned a lot about what she *didn't* want. As she buckles down to her online dating search, she does not feel pressured because she knows who she is: a fairly traditional woman with a strong desire to raise a family. Suzie is looking for a partner who is her intellectual equal and who will value companionship within a warm, supportive partnership. She knows she needs a stable guy, who has his feet on the ground to balance and complement her whimsical nature. Suzie's best prospects will be those whose personalities fall into the one or two boxes; four may also work, although this man may not challenge her enough.

Emilie, 42

Her score, 68 percent Alpha and 50 percent Beta, puts this single working mother of twin boys in the high Alpha/high Beta range (one). As such, Emilie, a glamorous and highly respected jewelry designer in New York City, combines a commanding presence with an intuitive grasp of feelings and relationships. She is adored in her business and worshiped by up-and-coming designers. Behind the scenes, her life has been difficult: she and her husband split when the twins were babies. She has not remarried and is raising the boys on her own. Emilie has tried online dating, but believes that her strong personality is off-putting to potential partners. With her European background, she is sophisticated and worldly. She is also outspoken—never hesitating to say exactly what she thinks, although politely prefacing it "with all due respect"—but tends to think herself less imposing than she actually is. Emilie tends to attract powerful Alpha men who compete with her. She has trouble with compromise, but has been working on it in therapy. Emilie needs a mellow guy with guts, someone who respects her natural hauteur but can push back and see past it to the warm, loving woman inside. A partner who falls into the one, two, four, or five box would be best.

DON'T BOX YOURSELF IN

When I asked Casey, a focus group participant who took the questionnaire (scoring mid Alpha/high Beta), how she felt about this method of personality and relationship evaluation, she said, "I came out slightly more Beta than Alpha, which *did* surprise me. But I don't see it as a negative."

Did you have a similar experience? Were you surprised by the results? Comforted? Confused? And what about the guys? Casey said that her boyfriend Dylan "initially wouldn't want to be called Beta; it would be a knee-jerk reaction. However, if I walked him through the questionnaire, he'd be fine. He identifies himself as a feminist, and he'd see himself in many of the positive Beta qualities."

Just remember: all Alphas need some Beta, and all Betas need some Alpha. The high Alpha woman has to learn to give up some control and tolerate greater vulnerability in order to make herself available for an emotional connection with a partner. She can use some Beta skills to become more sensitive and more of a team player. A high Beta woman can learn to take on typically Alpha tasks she's always shirked, like money; being more take-charge is definitely to her benefit.

So your score (or his) can tell you a great deal that is positive. At the same time, while the score tells you where you are now, you do *not* have to be boxed in. Pigeonholing people is not the idea! Instead, think of the questionnaire as an aspirational tool, to help you pinpoint areas to improve upon. With increased self-awareness, everyone does have the capacity to become more balanced.

CHAPTER 3

SEX AND THE ALPHA WOMAN

IT'S THE BEST OF all possible worlds. Women can have sex without making a commitment. They can delay marriage, have fun, and focus on their careers. They are sexually assertive, and when the time is right, they will meet and marry their Alpha male counterparts. True?

Well, it's complicated.

o   o   o   o

"The Alpha male is the desired man. These guys can pick and choose among the women." —*Molly*

"Alpha guys are totally into their jobs. There's no follow-through in relationships." —*Dani*

"It's fun to be around a guy who makes you nervous. I have this fantasy of being sexually ravished." —*Lori*

"Sexually, I have no trouble being assertive. I don't feel emotionally vulnerable in bed. It's asking for other stuff, like a guy's time; *that* makes me nervous." —*Serena*

"Alpha guys are *not* the most desirable. They're too focused on themselves. They're not relationship oriented. I finally met someone family oriented, as I am." —*Holly*

"I want both. You want to feel he's sexy and stronger than you are. But if that's all he is, it's so empty." —*Ann*

"We chase after these Alpha guys. You have this heart-pumping sex, but over time you miss out on bonding qualities. Next morning you want to hang out and cuddle, but by five AM he's left for the gym." —*Jamila*

"When I worked in banking, I was really attracted to Alpha males. Then I realized they were the mirror image of me. And they're incredibly self-absorbed! I realized I needed someone not like that at all. I ended up marrying a guy with a Beta heart and an Alpha penis! Oh—and by the way, I'm the one who goes out to the gym at five AM, and he's the one who complains!" —*Yvette*

○ ○ ○ ○

THE LURE OF THE ALPHA MALE

"I love Alpha guys because they're so sexy," says my client Emily, settling comfortably against the couch cushions. "I've been talking to this guy on OkCupid. He calls himself a real man," she adds with a mischievous smile.

"Emily," I say. "What are you thinking? If this is what he puts up front about himself, he's probably just another macho guy!"

Most things have come easily for Emily, a well-known CEO at an Internet start-up, and she's always assumed that when she was ready for marriage she'd meet her male counterpart: someone as ambitious and competitive as she is. In her early thirties and Asian American, she is self-confident, assertive, and unabashedly sexual. Although she's always envisioned herself married with children, she's been leading a freewheeling social life and totally enjoying it. But a yearlong relationship recently ended, and she entered therapy to understand why she hasn't met the right guy yet and to figure out what to do.

"I know. I know," she says. "But he's really cute and the sex will be great." She gives me a wide grin.

So much for the serious relationship she swears she wants!

"You know," she says now. "A lot of men I meet expect me to fit the stereotype of the docile Asian woman."

We both smile.

"Well, guess what, Dr. Rhodes," she says with emphasis. "I am not."

Frankly, Emily is a tiger. Her style is confrontational and feisty. A while ago, she told me a story about a man she went out with a few times. "We were always locking horns," she said. "One time when we went out to dinner, I challenged him about a racist comment he made to the waitress. As we got up to leave, he actually put his leg out and tripped me." She'd obviously been winning the argument.

Emily, a strong, passionate woman who owns her competitive and assertive nature, has reached a crucial turning point: she wants a long-term relationship. Still, as she admits a few sessions later, "I don't allow people in easily." Even as a child, she recalls, "I struggled to do everything for myself. I was self-sufficient and a perfectionist. I don't want to depend on anyone, because then they can disappoint me." As we talked some more, I suggested that she might choose men who are uncomfortable with intimacy so that it's easier to keep them at a distance. She became quiet as she considered this.

After several months of sorting out her unsuccessful relationships with the Alpha guys she's been attracted to, Emily is struggling with conflicting desires. "I really need to find someone less intense," she admits. "And not so domineering, a man with a gentler style. He doesn't have to be a killer on Wall Street; he just has to have a strong work ethic and be independent."

But sometimes she's still attracted to those Alphas, even though what she *doesn't* need now is the kind of guy who will ravish her in bed, but be unable and unwilling to build a real partnership. Been there; done that. What she does need is a guy who respects and admires her leadership qualities, her ambition, self-confidence, and success in the world—without considering her a threat. She needs someone assertive but not confrontational and emotionally accessible—a partner who is accomplished, but places a high value on relationships and great sex. Emily, a strong Alpha female, is heartily in need of a good Beta male. In fact, Beta men are the perfect catch for Alpha women like her.

SEXUAL STEREOTYPING

In the 1970s, evolutionary psychologists applied Darwinian theory to explain the differences in sexual behavior for men and women. They elaborated on the "evolutionary" differences in the sexes (men are hunters; women are gatherers) to explain the assumed natural adaptations that men seek power while women seek security, harkening back to Victorian times, when men were authoritarian and manly and women were passive and ladylike (and repressed). And this was only the beginning of the proliferation of the myths about gender differences. These notions fly in the face of today's sexual mores, but many people still adhere to the old ideas.

New research is challenging the idea that sex differences are ingrained, or that men are hardwired to be more sexual than women. After scrutinizing more than a dozen older studies on gender, personality, and behavior, researchers found that in a variety of attributes, including sexual attitudes and behavior, "men and women overlapped considerably." The authors went on to say that a belief in "categorical differences" between women and men actually doubles down on traditional stereotypes "by treating certain behaviors as immutable." Psychologist Janet Hyde's study concluded that most gender differences in sexual attitudes and behavior were small.

The fact is there is no evidence that raw sexuality is more masculine by nature, as opposed to nurture (cultural norms). Society has been narrowly defining gender behavior, and the emerging research is saying "hogwash!"

THE SEXUAL/EMOTIONAL SPLIT

"I want to get fucked!" proclaims my client Valerie, giving me a knowing smile. She's being deliberately outrageous, but I'm aware that she's expressing her genuine frustration about sex with her boyfriend Michael. "This guy may be too passive for me," she frets. From what I can tell from her description, Michael is a solid Beta with some Alpha—lower than most of her previous lovers.

Many women get trapped in what therapists call splitting, which is when you divide the world into black and white. A man either is aggressive, irresponsible, and sexy, *or* he is sensitive, responsible, and dorky in bed. The bad boy is hot but unreliable. The good guy is caring but uncool. Instead of integrating all the facets of a person into a composite whole, many women divide men into two categories, which makes finding a good match difficult.

Splitting is an *unconscious* strategy that helps deal with internal conflict. Many women are torn between their strong sexual desires (physical passion) and their relationship needs (emotions). Because these feel irreconcilable, women split off one or the other: a relationship is either all about emotions or it's all about sex. This doesn't sound right—and it isn't.

For Alpha women, there is a distinct twist. Generally, an Alpha will own her spirit of aggression and competitiveness in most areas of her life—but when it comes to sex she may be loath to take the initiative. Our culture hits women with these familiar double messages: be sexy, but don't be overtly sexual, and be eager, but don't be slutty. And then there's the dire warning that if you show an intense sexual appetite, you will emasculate your man. Let a man be the man in bed, women are taught. Is it any wonder, then, that in sexual encounters Alphas perceive their take-charge qualities as unfeminine, and shy away from being explicit about their needs? Is it so surprising that strong women want a man to take the sexual lead? It's paradoxical, and it's outdated—but some cultural norms die hard. Most women, Alphas as well as Betas, have a fantasy of an aggressive guy who takes them, sweeping them off to sexual ecstasy.

Valerie has never been ostensibly conflicted about so-called male and female attributes. She isn't shy about her sexual appetite—no shrinking violet she. She's been in a relationship with Michael for several months, but below the surface she has been wrestling with her ambivalence for some time now. An artist who's had some well-reviewed shows, Michael teaches at a prestigious art school in Manhattan. He's smart and worldly, and they share the same cultural interests—but he is less sexually experienced than she is.

With the Alpha men she dated, Valerie frequently ended up in competition and power plays, while she and Michael have a warm, companionable relationship and share the same vision of life. What Valerie appreciated most was Michael's mellow personality, in contrast to her driven, overcontrolling tendencies. Like Emily, she is looking for a man to marry and have a family with. Is Michael the one? She's attracted to him, and they always have sex on their frequent nights together, but she's disappointed. Still, she hesitates to ask for what she wants, and this is odd because she is usually very assertive. Why does this high Alpha shy away from pursuing her own pleasure?

She is exasperated that Michael isn't a mind reader. "I don't want to tell him what to do," she says, irritation in her voice. "I want him to know what I want him to do!"

With a laugh, she adds, "I want him to attack me sexually," and she isn't exactly kidding. On the other side of the coin for an assertive woman like Valerie are her sexual conflicts—the *Fifty Shades of Grey* syndrome—which lead her to be seduced by the idea of being taken, assuaging her fear that she is too male. Her assertiveness benefits her at work, but in bed she wants to feel feminine. She imagines being swept off her feet, tossed on the bed or backed up against the kitchen sink; the idea of having her clothes ripped off and arms pinned makes her feel female in a primal way. This dynamic resonates with Valerie, because, independent as she is in other realms, in bed she wants to be taken.

There's nothing wrong with that—but let her speak up about it! If you want to be ravished, then say so. Valerie can't expect her boyfriend to know, and she has to own up to her needs.

Many independent, assertive women associate raw sexuality with maleness, and the popularity of Brazilian waxing speaks to society's conflicts about female sexuality. I'm not going to beat around the bush about this: women want to please men, and women and men alike unconsciously want to neutralize women's power, so women tone themselves down, from strong adult women into dainty girls. This split between women's aggression and their sexual desires is contradictory; infantilizing yourself is not a way to resolve the problem.

One twenty-six-year-old woman told me why she and her friends are totally against it. "First, I don't see why women should go along with a porn-fueled male idea of what women should be," she said. "And second, ouch!"

Worse, not owning your own powerful sexuality may prevent you from being with a terrific Beta guy who may be a little inhibited in bed or who prefers tender sex to rough sex. If women sit and wait for men to intuit what they want, they will be forever grumpy, thwarted, and dissatisfied.

AVOID SEXUAL GUESSING GAMES

A twenty-nine-year-old woman in a focus group said, "You definitely have to let guys know what you expect. If you need him to amp it up, say so. When I first started having sex with one man, I put my vibrator on the headboard. He didn't use it, and I didn't say anything. Sometimes it's hard to do that in the moment. The second time, he did use it. If he hadn't I would have said something. It would have been up to me."

On the issue of oral sex, two women commented on another woman's problem with a boyfriend who didn't go down on her. She gave him blow jobs, though. "That's *wrong*," Toni said. Her friend Holly added, "I'd be patient if he said, 'Give me more time.' If he still didn't want to do it, it wouldn't be a deal breaker, as long as there were other ways I could come. But if that was the only way, it *could* be the deal breaker."

Everyone knows men like blow jobs, but it's also true that many refuse to go down on women. A man may have no problem asking for what he wants in bed, but if he is reluctant to give back (and feels entitled not to), a woman should speak up about the imbalance between giving and taking. Our culture still allows men much more latitude than it allows women in expressing their sexual desires. Women then fall into the trap of thinking they need to satisfy their man. Even Alpha women will need to make a conscious effort to reject the old-fashioned idea that nice girls don't like sex, and ask for what they want. In my clinical experience with men, I find that most do want thoughtful feedback from women (if they don't want it, they are selfish and should not be in your bed). Men who are not threatened by Alpha women are turned on when women are explicit about their needs; they want to hear from you. When you don't speak out, as you so freely do in other areas of your life, it can only be due to some buried guilt and shame that you experience about your sexual appetite. And that is a real shame!

"IT'S ALL HIS FAULT"

From early on in her relationship with Michael, Valerie tended to focus on his flaws. "You are making it all about him, as if all the problems are his," I pointed out. "You may be pushing him away because of your own difficulty with closeness." Not that he was perfect, but I'd noticed that whenever she was uncomfortable over their growing intimacy, she focused on his problems, never her own. That told me something important about what was going on in the relationship.

Alpha females tend to blame others more than Betas do. In psychological parlance, it's a typical example of projection: you externalize your issues and accuse the other person of having the problem. (Betas tend to blame themselves for problems, sexual or otherwise.) Because I knew how well Valerie could rise to a challenge, I posed it to her this way: Why was she being so uncharacteristically passive? Why was she distancing herself from her own power and self-confidence? And why was she not looking at her own role in their dynamic?

Her responsibility was to let Michael know that she wanted more variety and more adventurous sex. Michael is sincere, interesting, and cautious—overall, a caring Beta guy with enough Alpha to assert his needs. The real question was: could he adapt to her sexual needs without being threatened by her Alpha? She wouldn't know unless she tried. She needed to choose the right moment to talk to him. Then she had to discuss the issue without being critical (tough for an Alpha); I advised her to use a light, playful touch when she brought up sex and to be consistent. And she had to openly share her fantasies, so that Michael understood her sexual needs and preferences. She needed to make the point that she wanted them to have sex the way she liked it as well as the way he did.

When I pointed out that it was fine for her to be the Alpha in the relationship, sexually and otherwise, she was surprised. It was a novel idea. As she began to relax into the evolving closeness of the relationship, it struck her that they'd reached a level of intimacy she'd never experienced before. She found that they could talk, and that sex did become more exciting. She also found satisfaction from experiencing a more tender side of sex.

Every woman deserves a great sex life. If the guy is a good Beta, and you are attracted to him but sex is lackluster, you should take the lead in bed. There is everything right about initiating and sharing your fantasies. You will then find out if he is a good enough Beta guy to accommodate your Alpha.

NICE GUY, BAD SEX?

Britney and James had been married for three years when she came to see me. From the day they met, she'd liked James—a nice guy who was successful and responsible. He'd fallen hard for her, too, and they'd enjoyed each other's company. After finding that they shared many of the same values about family, they quickly became a couple. "I knew he was someone who would always have my back," she said, correctly perceiving him to be a caretaker, a Beta man through and through, and the polar opposite of all the bad boys she'd always been attracted to.

But there was one tiny problem. "He is so nice, and I really love him, but sex was always an issue. It's boring and there's no chemistry at all," she explained. She'd married him in spite of her awareness of their sexual incompatibility, because she'd felt secure and cared for. Now in a sexless marriage, she was in a pickle.

I questioned why she'd gone ahead with the marriage when she'd known something was wrong.

"I felt like I made a rational choice," she argued. "There are so many good things about him and one bad thing." This was interesting, and almost persuasive, but ultimately it didn't add up, because the one bad thing turned out to be huge.

Huge. Britney didn't listen to her gut; instead she "split." Nice guy, bad sex—and even though she was here in my office, looking miserable, she was still trying to convince herself (and me) that sexual dysfunction didn't matter. Before their wedding, she'd had episodes of doubt but had pushed these feelings aside. It is normal to get the jitters when you're about to walk down the aisle, but sometimes these doubts indicate deeper trouble. If a woman has cold feet about a serious issue like sex, she should not discount it. She should share her concerns with a trusted friend or see a therapist for a reality check. Going into marriage in a state of denial over something major has big implications: some recent research shows that doubting women have a higher divorce rate than doubting men, suggesting that women's doubts have more substance.

When she was in her twenties, Britney, an Alpha woman with a deep Beta side (she has a strong need to be taken care of) worked in advertising; she loved the office environment and prospered professionally and socially. But she'd ended up with men who mistreated her.

After each painful relationship, she felt abandoned and vulnerable—experiences that mirrored the sense of loss she'd felt as a teenager when her mother died in a car crash.

Now, at thirty-five, Britney was panicking. "What should I do?" she asked. When I replied that she could teach James how to make love she got squeamish. "Oh no," she said. "That wouldn't work."

Unlike Valerie, who was attracted to Michael, Britney was not attracted to James. In fact, she dreaded sex.

And that was when I knew the relationship was at a dead end. If basic chemistry is missing, taking the lead or trying new techniques feels strange and artificial. You have to be attracted to each other before you challenge yourself to initiate or tinker with the technical aspects of sex. And it is hard to create chemistry if it was not there in the beginning.

"But it isn't really that important," she insisted. "And doesn't sex mean less as you get older? We really get along and we want to have kids."

"Sex is very important in a relationship," I said. "And it gets even more important as people get older. Being sexual keeps you young and attached to your partner. You're a very sexual person, Britney, so sex will always mean a lot to you. This is why you came to see me," I reminded her.

She invited James to a couple's session. He was acutely aware that she'd been withdrawn and uninterested in sex (it had been six months since they'd last slept together), but he had no idea what was wrong. When she blurted it out in the session, he froze to his seat, flabbergasted and hurt. When a secret of this magnitude is divulged in treatment, it is always very painful, leaving the participants—including the therapist—drained and exhausted.

For Britney, it was a huge relief to confess the truth. And painful as it was, it was the right thing to do if they were ever to get out of their rut. In an individual session a few days later, James confessed how dev-astated he'd been. He admitted he'd been making excuses to himself for their lack of a sex life, but he loved Britney and held out hope that they could work it out. He was ready to "do anything," but he would not settle for a sexless marriage.

I told James that he deserved to be with someone who was attracted to him, and though he was wounded now, I had no doubt that if he and Britney couldn't work things out, he'd find a woman who'd love him for his many wonderful qualities.

Usually, I coach couples to talk through their problems and work on re-creating what was once the glue between them. If there is sexual energy, as there is between Valerie and Michael, I encourage them to exchange sexual fantasies. I believe that if Britney and James had had children right away, they would have stayed together and jointly put sex on the back burner while focusing on the kids. But the marriage would have deteriorated over time, because a sexless marriage is usu-ally not sustainable. Even if a marriage starts out with a ton of chem-istry, sex can get stale over time and the couple will have to work on keeping their attraction alive. If you start out without chemistry, well, there's not much even the best therapist can do.

The takeaway is crystal clear: listen to your gut. If Britney had done so, she'd have known not to ignore something as important as sexual dysfunction. But she'd squelched her self-doubts and had never told a soul about her sexual ennui until the day she stepped into my office.

Then she flew into a panic at the thought of staying in the mar-riage *and* of leaving it. "If I leave James, what will happen?" she asked. She was afraid she'd go back to dating the kind of Alpha guys who'd treated her so poorly in the past.

In order for her to put to bed her bad choices of bad boys, Britney needed to understand why she'd chosen them. Together, we worked on her gaining insight into how those experiences echoed the pain she'd felt when her mother died. Gradually, she came to see that a relationship does not have to cause or end in pain, whether the pain stemmed from the abandonment that was part of her earlier choices or from the deprivation she suffered with James.

"You can make better choices now," I told her. "This is hard, but you have the capacity to do it. And my hunch is that you'll find someone your own age or possibly an older guy who'd love a beautiful, independent woman like you. Someone who'll be all over you— think of that! Or, if you don't get married, you can still have a life you want. You can plan for a future, with or without marriage."

Once we discussed her choices, Britney began the difficult process of seeing her life not in terms of black or white, either/or, but instead as filled with possibilities far more interesting and varied than she'd ever imagined.

As a Beta catch, James will have an easier time transitioning out of the marriage. Most likely, he will end up with someone who is modest in her sexual needs, and someone with whom he does not have to worry about the ticking biological clock. Britney, as a woman in her midthirties who wants children, is more vulnerable, but she is resilient and independent. I believe that she will grow from her mistake and find the right path.

BAD GUY, GOOD SEX?

Will great sex necessarily lead to a great relationship? If only. When Jenna was introduced to Jake at a Super Bowl party, she felt an immediate thrill. Once she realized she'd known him in high school, she could hardly believe he was the same guy. An Alpha male had emerged from the cocoon of a teenage nerd. Somewhere along the way, he'd grown taller than she was—she was tall and willowy—successful in business, and extremely attractive. They chatted throughout the evening, and the electricity crackled. After the party, they texted and, two days later, had a great hookup. After that came a flurry of texts, which she responded to immediately and then—unbearable radio silence all the next week. "I thought we really hit it off," she told me, disappointed and confused.

Jenna could play a character in a TV series about a sexy, successful young woman leading a charmed life in the Big Apple. Now in her early thirties, she was getting plenty of positive buzz about her new entrepreneurial venture and until recently had been enjoying a casual, freewheeling sex life. But Jenna was at a turning point. She'd become dissatisfied with hookups and the men she was meeting. She'd enjoyed some casual sex, but that was getting old, and she'd begun to feel that she wanted a partner, not a fling.

Several weeks later, after she'd reluctantly given up on him, a text from Jake popped up. He asked her to come over, and Jenna jumped into a cab. At his apartment, they ate takeout and tumbled into bed, which led to a series of passionate hookups over the course of a couple of weeks. She felt certain that their natural chemistry extended further than sex; they shared easy, funny conversations and lots of interests. When he started dropping things like "I bet our children will be math whizzes" and "this summer, we should take a house together," she was even more turned on. Then she didn't hear from him for three weeks. This was the moment when Jenna could have saved herself a lot of grief by realizing that they wanted different things from life and moving on.

When Jake finally texted her again, she immediately called him and demanded to know what was going on. To her relief he pinned down an actual date ("let's have dinner on Monday," which was three days off), only to cancel by text at the last minute because of "work pressures." So much for that!

He went on to cancel twice more with flimsy excuses, along the lines of "the dog ate my homework," which Jenna, in her addled state, accepted. She liked him so much she couldn't face the real message. Like many Alpha women, Jenna is typically quicker to anger than to feeling hurt and rejected, but in her session she was uncharacteristically teary. "I just know there's something more to this relationship," she insisted.

"There's no excuse for three times in a row," I said bluntly. "Let's try to figure out what's going on." I suggested that the texting pattern might be a high-tech form of the revenge of the nerd, the behavior of an awkward teenager who returns to the dating scene to jerk around the popular girl out of resentment toward all the desirable women who'd once rejected him.

Jenna shook her head emphatically. She was so hung up on him and so determined to make it work that she ignored the obvious signs that he was not available for more than a casual relationship. She could not accept that she was being victimized; on some level, she simply could not imagine failure. "He's clueless; that's all," she defended him in one session.

Not so much clueless as cruel. I saw how hurt she was, and I pointed out that she needed to own her vulnerability. By continuing to let him lead her on, she was fending off facing the intolerable (to her) fact that she was helpless. It is extremely hard for a high Alpha to admit loss of control and helplessness. "He doesn't mean to hurt me," she asserted. Whether he meant it or not, he *was* hurting her. Giving one false positive cue after another is a form of torture.

"I think you're cutting him way too much slack because you like him so much," I said. "And, because you hate feeling the loss of control, you keep fighting to make the relationship happen. You don't like to take no for an answer."

In this case, a woman's strong Alpha qualities—resilience, determination, and overconfidence—worked against her. In Jenna's brand of splitting, she denied her emotional needs. It made her unable to see that while they had a lot in common, many important things were missing: stability, honesty, reliability, and true caring.

CHAPTER 4

BACHELORS, BOYFRIENDS,
AND MARRIED MEN

THE SINGLE MOST IMPORTANT decision you will ever make is choosing the right partner. You can marry someone who will create havoc in your life or someone who will join you in forging a great partnership. And the choice is yours.

There's an upside and a downside to looking for a relationship right now. On the upside, we're entering an age of a new ideal of masculinity, which is based on the ability to be a great husband/partner and father, instead of on the notion of dominance and "mine is bigger than yours." Beta men have happily accepted the rise of successful, empowered women by defining themselves differently from the traditional male of years past. A man with solid Beta qualities is ahead of the curve; he is adapting to a changing reality.

On the downside, well, there's a lot of confusion about gender roles. What I will provide here are the tools to help you understand how men are dealing with the transition, how to read different kinds of behavior, and how to assess a guy's ability to partner with a strong woman.

EMOTIONAL TRUTHS

I have always worked with men as well as women, and I love the fact that my practice is so welcoming to men. I like and respect men, which is a real asset in my business. With couples, as you might suspect, therapy is usually initiated by the woman—but the awesome challenge of my work is to engage the reluctant male. A few years ago, when I was redecorating my office, I asked my husband's opinion of the color I was planning to use on the walls. "Too pink! Too feminine!" he exclaimed. "Your men will not like it." (Actually, it was peach, not pink.) I realized I actually *was* aiming for a subtly feminized environment, in which men could feel less macho and more emotional. In that peachy office, they confide in me as a sister, a mother, a wife (and yes, eventually they do talk about their feelings!).

Just as most women are developing Alpha qualities, most men are developing Beta tendencies. As women and men move away from traditional gender roles at the extremes on the continuum, we're all in flux. After several months of therapy, an Alpha in his forties opened up to me about the pain of his early childhood that included his father's alcoholism and abusiveness. As a successful athlete in college and a lawyer at a prestigious law firm, my client had always described his childhood as a suburban Connecticut idyll. At some point I became aware that he was profoundly lonely in his marriage; he seemed to expect very little companionship or support from his wife. I wondered out loud if the loneliness didn't echo how he'd felt as a child. Nourished and affirmed by his success in the outside world, he unconsciously re-created the deprivations of his childhood by staying in an unhappy marriage. As he explored the disappointment and loneliness, he realized that he wanted more, and was willing to work hard to break old patterns.

Another client, who prided himself on projecting an image of control and power, admitted to me his worries about his health. He had palpitations but had never mentioned this, or his sense of vulnerability, to anyone. Although he was only in his midfifties, mortality had raised its ugly head in the consciousness of this larger-than-life Alpha male.

It is not unusual for men to cry in my office. One man, grieving his father's imminent death from cancer, broke down in tears. "I can't let him go," he said. He felt guilty for not loving his father enough and helpless that he could not take away his father's pain from cancer. Another man admitted that he felt like a "cash cow" with his children—that they valued him only for his wealth.

While women will usually talk out problems with friends, men will present a stoic front. They're supposed to be tough—and it's unrealistic. That's why, when a man shares his private worries and insecurities, I feel I am witnessing something very personal and meaningful. It's a huge responsibility to mirror these feelings and make our relationship a sanctuary. The spell is sometimes broken when, uncomfortable with the intensity of emotions, he assures me that the issue he's talking about is no big deal. But I know we have inched closer to experiencing real closeness, and my hope is that he can do the same in his intimate relationships.

During the recent recession, I saw many couples whose marital crises were mired in a breadwinner husband's loss of income. Having lost their sense of agency, these men were humiliated and broken. Many could not bear to tell their wives that they had to cut down on spending: each man, to a one, felt as if he were letting his wife down. I had to encourage men to level with their wives. Easier said than done: they hesitated because of shame stemming from the loss of stature.

These sessions were extremely painful as couples grappled not only with a whole new economic reality but also with the vast ripple effect on their relationships. But there is no avoiding the new reality. As the culture changes, men are feeling squeezed. Who *are* you if your wife outshines you? Who *are* you if you are not the breadwinner? Who *are* you without your job? How do you redefine yourself? How do you rebuild and sustain an identity while cultural tides are eroding the ground you stand on? Many men are harnessing Beta qualities as the most helpful way to meet this challenge. These qualities allow men to ask for support, approach challenges through a partnership, and create an identity that is not dependent on the old-fashioned notion: I work; therefore I am.

I try to make my office a safe place for men and women alike to share their feelings of vulnerability, helplessness, disappointment, and unhappiness. It is my responsibility to allow people to expose their so-called weaknesses and pain. In a helpful therapeutic process, the development of trust allows people not to feel stripped of their dignity when they expose their innermost thoughts.

ARE MEN THREATENED BY STRONG WOMEN?

Yes, some men are. Others are enamored of strong women. As one man, married to an Alpha, put it: "You have to have a strong ego to be with an Alpha woman." A guy needs the ego strength to play orchestra to a woman's conductor. To understand how a man develops it, you need to take a look at the early personal history that men in our culture share. Those experiences influence how men envision women and how they develop relationships with the women in their lives.

As a boy emerges from infancy into boyhood, he begins to self-identify as a male. Many experiences combine to create that identity: his relationship with his father; the degree of closeness and respect between his parents; his other role models (grandmothers, grandfathers, uncles, aunts); the family culture (woman friendly? misogynistic?); and, last but not least, his relationship with his mother (in traditional marriages, the primary parent). If she was a controlling, domineering (negative) Alpha mom, his struggle for autonomy will be more difficult. His feelings toward her will be ambivalent, and he will spend much psychic energy defining himself in *opposition* to her. Later in his life, he will be ultrasensitive to controlling women and possibly even misogynistic. This man always needs his space and chafes at women telling him what to do.

Even though it's safe to say that male insecurity lies at the root of the fear of strong women, the guy with a perfectly healthy ego may also have a knee-jerk reaction to a directive woman. If you're Alpha, your tone and word choice may skew toward sounding bossy and condescending; after all, you're accustomed to being in charge. So, should you tone yourself down to assuage a man's ego? Maybe.

Toning yourself down implies taking your Alpha away, which I would never suggest. But try to become more self-observant and choose a different tone and communication style. If it's in your nature to be strong and directive, it's up to you to take the lead in modifying an interactional pattern that doesn't work. By doing so, you aren't transforming yourself into someone you're not. But if you've ever noticed a guy bristle when you're speaking to him or seen the scuff marks on the floor as he digs in his heels, you need to develop an ear for your tone of voice and the words you choose, and try not to be dogmatic or critical. You'll need to tune your radar in to his reactions: we don't like it when men are controlling, and men get defensive when women do the same.

As gender roles transform and fathers take an increasingly active role in child rearing, the boy's mommycentric world is opening up to include a strong, loving male parenting figure. This child's world is more balanced and less scary. And I think this kind of experience will give rise to men who are less likely to be fearful of strong women. And isn't it about time?

YOUR WAY OR THE HIGHWAY?

"I make the money in the family, so I deserve to have things my way." It is the rare Alpha woman who so blatantly equates power with income, but it *does* happen. Usually Alpha women assert power in other ways, which are also alienating. She may rule the roost by bossing her partner around in front of other people, which is both impolite and embarrassing to *everyone*. One Alpha client was quick to pick a fight when her partner, a great Beta guy, chose to stay at home finishing a project instead of meeting her after work. Watch out for my-way-or-the-highway Alpha behavior.

Put some useful Beta skills into play: ask questions instead of issuing edicts. One Alpha and her Beta boyfriend were discussing something that had upset him at work. His boss had criticized his approach with a client and he disagreed—strongly. In a superior tone she chided him that he became defensive whenever he was criticized.

Even though you may be an excellent problem solver, hold the advice; it could be deadly. Instead of telling him what he does wrong, listen carefully. Be sympathetic. Then you might ask: Was there any merit in the criticism at all? Anything that might actually be useful? You might add that you know how hard it is to take criticism; most people—including you!—find it difficult.

The interaction should be positive: he's confiding in you, which is a sure sign of intimacy and trust. Put yourself in his shoes, and recognize that it isn't easy for him to confide without feeling vulnerable. By being empathic you're creating an environment in which uncomfortable feelings may be shared. This is the cornerstone of intimacy.

If a man seems *particularly* sensitive to directives, you need to understand why. This is where your "observing ego" comes into play: the capacity to stand back and watch yourself. When one woman's husband complained that she was in the driver's seat in their relationship, she was puzzled because she'd never seen herself as bossy. Ask him for specifics and do a reality check with friends who know you well. You may be bossier than you think, or he may be extrasensitive.

Frankly, most men *are* a little oppositional; this is usually not a big problem if you both have a sense of humor and don't get into giant power struggles.

BETA—OR OMEGA?

A group of women I interviewed claimed that they eliminated any prospective dating candidate who said he took yoga classes. They'd suspect him of falsely advertising himself as sensitive and spiritual.

"Not the ones who come to my yoga class," I replied. "In fact, they're hot." Women have a hard time distinguishing between the highly desirable Beta guy and the Omega loser. And doing yoga is not the way to tell the difference!

The Omega guy has been around forever, not just since the economic downturn. He is the ultimate narcissist, feeling entitled to live off anyone who will support him and make little, if any, contribution to the household. He may play video games all day, drink an excessive amount of beer, surf the net, and generally enshrine his adolescence. He has no job with which to self-identify and looks down on working stiffs. Do not—ever—confuse the Beta darling with the Omega leech. They are quite different.

OMEGA · A dreamer. He is still in a band that's going to make it big; a talented writer who will, one day, when he gets over his block, write the great American novel—on Twitter; gifted but unappreciated by the world; spends most of his day "networking" with pals from college who are in pretty much the same boat as he is.

BETA · A dreamer *and* a doer. He has a great work ethic and a strong sense of self; refuses to give excuses for not trying; can accept and learn from criticism. Realistic enough to move on if something doesn't pan out.

OMEGA · Allergic to work. He defines himself in opposition to the work world, which he feels is too cutthroat for his sensibilities; won't compromise his standards in his quest to find himself; won't pitch in; lets dishes pile up and dust bunnies take over; turns over with a groan as you rush out to work.

BETA · Finds the work world tough but gamely faces adversity. He may not be wildly ambitious, but has a strong work ethic; if unemployed, picks up the chores at home; if creative, makes a structure for himself; has a strong enough ego to maintain a sense of self in the real world.

OMEGA · He's either too fragile or too high-and-mighty to accommodate to external demands; prides himself on his artistic soul and high "standards."

BETA · Thinks things through, resilient, dependable. He knows what has to get done—and does it! If knocked down, he gets back up.

OMEGA · Identifies as a victim. Defiant. He won't take orders from *anyone*; may have substance abuse issues.

BETA · Understands that bosses will tell him what to do. He knows it may be grinding and difficult, but accepts that as a middle manager he will report to someone higher up.

ENABLING THE NOWHERE MAN

Speaking of Omegas, I've found that many strong women become enmeshed with very needy men, creating a complex, mutually dependent relationship. My motto (and it should be theirs!) is: having it all does not mean doing it all. Enabling is extreme caretaking. You are very competent and can manage many things and support many people. It is all too easy for your competence to work against you—and before you know it, you've become an enabler.

When you first hear the word *enabling*, you may visualize a long-suffering martyr or a passive doormat sacrificing her life and sanity to an alcoholic or drug-addicted partner, unknowingly supporting his self-destructive behavior. But enabling doesn't necessarily involve substance abuse. It also happens when you expect less of your partner than what that person is capable of. If you're in a relationship in which you seem to be carrying the burden of work and household chores, you're settling for less than you want or deserve—to the extreme. Enabled partners will suck the life out of you.

A couple I knew was a classic case. The husband, an artist, was married to a tenured university professor who carried a full course load. She was well respected in her field and in demand as a lecturer. The couple rarely saw each other because he worked at night in his studio while she slept, and they lived in a symbiotic bubble in which she kept them afloat, financially, emotionally, and physically. When a friend finally asked to see his work—maybe he *was* a genius—he said no, that he was not prepared to let anyone see. He was developing his style.

What exactly was she getting from the relationship? I think she believed in his talent, but used it as a way to rationalize his behavior. Underneath, her terror of abandonment drove her to demand so little from him. How better to avoid abandonment than by enabling a dependent partner without any resources to leave? To assuage her fear, she needed him to be fully dependent and nonfunctional. Their relationship was a cocoon of mutual dependency.

Both partners were low Beta, low Alpha. The woman's competence and talents pulled her Alpha up enough to allow her to succeed in the outside world, but she was emotionally crippled by her fears. For both partners, their unhealthy arrangement served as a buffer against personal and professional challenges.

An Alpha or a Beta woman can fall into this trap. If you grew up as the parent of your parents, you were what is called a parentified child. In this role you assumed responsibilities beyond your developmental age because your parents were for any of a number of reasons unable to perform them. As a child one Alpha woman cared for her ill parents and held the family together through one crisis after another. Everyone relied on her ability to be the family linchpin. As an adult she applied those hard-won managerial skills to her career and and became a top manager at a publishing company, although she carried a heavy toll in her personal life.

Many Alpha enablers leave work, stop to pick up groceries, arrive at home, and start making dinner. This gender deviation neutralization, as sociologists call it, reflects a woman's role conflict: without realizing it, she is compensating for crossing into the breadwinner role and being too masculine. In reality, there is no acknowledgment that the family depends on her bringing home the bacon *and* serving it for dinner. Thankless! And eventually, you will get tired of being and doing everything.

Because Betas tend to sit on their anger and mask it as depression, a Beta enabler may be unaware that she is mad as hell. As a lawyer, Jillian took her work seriously and made a great salary, but when she consulted with me, she was no longer taking joy or pleasure in anything. Her background was very hard: the family had been poor and her mother psychotic, leaving Jillian essentially orphaned, never acknowl-edged or appreciated. Nonetheless she got herself through college and law school and married Bill, who at that time was a historian who liked to dabble in antiques collecting. He was playful and charming, and she felt that she'd pulled herself up by her bootstraps into a very good life. Jillian was shy and tended to take the backseat. Bill was her ticket to sociability and she was his ticket to a reality-based, solvent life.

When Bill quit teaching to devote himself to antiques dealing, Jil-lian worked more hours to make up for the loss of salary. They shared the housework fairly equally. The two of them spoke often of moving to upstate New York and opening a bed-and-breakfast that Bill would furnish with vintage treasures he'd collected. Jillian would run the business and he would entertain guests with his inimitable bonhomie.

But as Bill's buying trips turned into extravagant outings in which he ended up spending more money buying collectibles than he did sell-ing them, things unraveled. No matter how hard Jillian worked, they couldn't save, and she felt trapped in the cycle of work without reward. She felt like a beast of burden, and she'd periodically lose her temper with him, but they'd gloss it over and go back to their routines. I told her that her occasional outbursts let some air out, without really chang-ing the status quo.

As it is with many Betas or people with strong Beta tendencies, Jillian was uncomfortable with anger, and depression became a cop-ing strategy. (Depression is anger turned inward.) It is safer to be self-critical and self-blaming than to put the anger out there. This is the cornerstone of depression.

We had a breakthrough one day. With great embarrassment, she told me that often, while she rode the subway to work, she fantasized herself as a celebrity and that all eyes were on her in awe and admira-tion. We figured it out together. "How does the fantasy make you feel?" I asked.

"I feel *visible*," she immediately replied. "While in my real life I usually feel *in*visible."

I encouraged her: "You want to be counted, to have a voice and be recognized. You deserve to be seen."

In our culture being a celebrity is the ultimate achievement: you're in the spotlight, admired and adored, beautiful and beloved, envied and worshiped. I was very touched by Jillian's fantasy, which was both humble and filled with yearning for something she desperately needed.

"How do you think you can be a star in your own life?" I asked her.

"I can't. I'm the worker bee in my marriage. I feel like a drone," she said.

We agreed that any good partner needs to bring more to the party than, in Bill's case, his charm. It wasn't easy, but Jillian took on the challenge and pushed her Beta personality toward direct, ongoing discussions with Bill. By dealing directly with her anger, she was harnessing her inner Alpha. When she brought her feelings out of the depths and articulated them, her depression began to lift, and the couple began to work at seriously saving money and planning for a real, not fantasized, future. And, to my question about how she could be the star of her own life, *that* proved to be the answer.

"IS HE GAY?"

I hear this question at least once a week as a woman ponders a man she's started dating. If he isn't a traditional Alpha and doesn't toss her on the bed and rip off her clothes on the first date, he must be gay, right? Wrong. It doesn't mean that at all. But women worry because we're in a transitional stage of gender roles, shifting away from tradition. It's a little sneaky thought lurking in the back of women's minds.

Maybe he isn't very aggressive, or he's a little too neat (picks up his towels and socks!). Maybe he seems too relationship oriented. Something about this bothers you. Is he a gay man who plans to marry a woman so he can "pass"? Or are his sexual conflicts hidden even from himself?

The entire staff at a women's magazine was gossiping about the new, handsome male creative director. Male employees are relatively unusual in their world. Was he gay? Was he not gay? They scrutinized the way he walked and talked, what he wore, and exactly how his shirt hit his hips. They concluded that yes, he was gay. As it turned out, he was not.

When women turn on their gaydar, it's often because they fear being taken in and making a mistake about a potential mate. They perceive a threat to their judgment, their sexuality, and their attractiveness. In the old days gay men and women tried to pass by making hetero marriages. For many gays, those bad old days are over. Still, plenty of men in culturally conservative communities try to hide their sexual orientation and will date women, even if it's difficult for them.

In the vast majority of cases, though, if a man is interested in you, rest assured; he's not gay. Keep in mind that gay males are aware of their orientation since before puberty, so you can bet your life that an adult man will be perfectly aware that he's gay. But things are changing, and we're naturally confused and anxious, worrying about who is legitimately male. Can a guy be a so-called real man, even if he's not overtly macho? Can he be genuinely hetero even if he's sensitive and— gasp—well dressed?

Yes, of course. Still, women wonder about men who don't seem sexually aggressive enough. When a woman asks me this question, I usually ask, "What makes you think so?" In the last five years I have never heard a good answer to this question. Then I say, "If he's gay, why in the world would he be interested in you?"

Betas and Alphas both worry about this, but the Alpha woman worries more, especially about sex. She is more tuned-in to dominant qualities. If he isn't sexually aggressive, then what is he? What if he can't satisfy her sexually? Many Alpha women are attracted to Alpha males who share their own qualities of competitiveness and dominance. They may be turned off at the thought of a man not being aggressive enough; they want to be deeply desired in a primal way, to be overwhelmed, swept away, tossed mightily on the bed, fucked against the kitchen counter.

None of these desires are unusual or wrong, but when you're ready to find a partner, don't limit yourself to the obvious prototypes. Beware the Omega, victimized by the world. Unhealthy enmeshment awaits you. Enjoy the Alpha, but consider whether he is your best partner. For someone who will work with you to build a life together and encourage you on your individual path, be it the PTA, academia, your own business, or Wall Street, the Beta man is the stand-up guy.

BACHELOR BEHAVIOR, EXPLAINED

I've seen lots of different kinds of guy behavior, and everyone is unique, but for the sake of convenience I've sketched out three general categories. If you're looking for a serious relationship, hone your instinct for reading behavior. The better you learn to read it, the better the choices you'll make, and the less time and emotional energy you'll expend.

The player

If you're an Alpha, you're attracted to your male counterpart because he's a challenge; if you're a Beta, you like Alpha men because they're fun and exciting. Players certainly aren't new—but now they're getting a free ride from casual digital communications. Booty calls are their specialty. They love apps like Tinder, which locate people in their vicinity who are available for quick, efficient sex.

In the eighties, I coauthored a book called *Cold Feet: Why Men Don't Commit*. Men were having problems adjusting to the independent women created by seventies' feminism. The trend, which I saw repeatedly in my practice, was that men both craved and feared intimacy, and women didn't know how to read the mixed signals. It was at first hard to distinguish who was a player and who was legitimate relationship material. Now technology makes it even harder, because the means of communication are so much faster and more elusive.

More men are staying single longer, and they can be spotted all about town, heads up and smartphones on. They are proud, sexy, and charming, and they're having the time of their lives in a culture where sex is free and women are cool. At a focus group of single men in their thirties and forties, whom I'd selected out as players, I asked if any of them were in relationships or planning on getting married in the near future. To a man they replied absolutely not. As one put it, "I'm having too much fun."

Tips: Players come in all shapes and sizes. So how do you spot them? Read a guy's pattern of relationships, or more accurately, the lack thereof. He is enjoying the world of no-penalty sex, with its infinite number of available women who get younger as he gets older. Is he a relationship prospect? Of course not. The typical Alpha player is fun for the short term, but won't be reliable over the long haul. Remember: it isn't what he *says*; it's what he *does*. Enjoy him but don't try to change his stripes!

The happily unhitched

At one time a never-married, forty-year-old man was viewed with suspicion, but no more. Paul, in his early forties, is neither an oddball nor gay. His mother confessed she's worried that Paul is lonely, but I assure her he isn't. He doesn't say anything to her about his personal life; he considers it private. A doting uncle to his siblings' kids, Paul works at home as a consultant. He has time to cook and garden on his terrace. Every day he walks his dog in the park and mixes in the social scene at the dog runs—some of the best spots in New York City to meet people. Plus, he meets women online. Women like him; he is obviously a good prospect. Married friends try to fix him up with fabulous single women they know—but Paul resists. The idea of being obligated turns him off.

Tips: Guys like Paul feel no internalized pressure to change the status quo. He dates when he feels like it, but he isn't a player. He is responsible, considerate, and enjoys dating and the company of women. He intends to be hitched—someday—but won't make the kinds of moves you might expect him to. Don't hesitate to take the lead; he needs it and wants it. But be his friend, not his boss, or he'll dig in his heels and resist. This guy can be an enigma: give him three months, and if he isn't seeing you regularly (at least twice a week), move on. He may be low-hanging fruit—but not quite ripe for the picking.

Josh, a postdoc scientist in his early thirties, was self-sufficient and very professionally ambitious. When he wasn't in the lab, he played in a band or went hiking or scuba diving. One day, Kathy, a brainy new research assistant, showed up in the lab. She chatted him up, and they became buddies. Soon he took her to his favorite hiking and rock-climbing haunts and then on a scuba diving expedition in fifty-degree water near San Francisco (a test perhaps?). He was threatened neither by her brains nor her adventurous spirit; in fact, he was totally impressed. He looked up to her and desired her but was too shy to initiate. Inexperienced in dating, he thought—although he wasn't absolutely sure—that she considered him as just a friend. But one day, tired of waiting for him to do something, she grabbed him and kissed him. He was thrilled to realize that she had romantic and sexual feelings toward him.

Guys like Josh can be a little clueless; don't interpret their behavior as a lack of interest. If you like him, hang in there—and take the lead. (Josh and Kathy got married two years after the first kiss.)

The serial monogamist

This one's a tough nut to crack. He appears to be a player, but isn't. At the same time he may *seem* more ready for a relationship than he really is. His behavior is earmarked by the way he throws himself into a monogamous relationship—for six months or so. It ends just as the woman starts expecting more. Even when he knows she's not for him, he doesn't mind letting things unravel slowly because he enjoys the drama and the great makeup sex.

A thirty-eight-year-old Alpha guy, with Beta warmth and attentiveness, Ian is respectful of women's intelligence and accomplishments. The glaring flaw in his personality is that he is looking for the perfect woman: beautiful, smart, accomplished, sexy, independent, and totally devoted to him. Women perceive him as interested in marriage—and he is, but maybe not in their lifetime. In his wake, he leaves a trail of women—mostly strong Alphas from whom he requires absolute devotion. Nor does he want a traditional Beta; he wants a woman to be independent and successful. In other words, he wants an autonomous woman who will wait on him hand and foot. He seems to be in love with an oxymoron.

Tips: My general rule is that by a year of steady dating, you should feel confident about where the relationship is headed. However, when you're thirty-three, thirty-four, thirty-five, or older, you want to avoid wasting even six months of your life on a guy who ultimately is going to bail. By then, he knows you well enough, but he may be looking around the corner for someone "better" or "perfect." Tune in to these clues: When you bring up the future, does he emit mixed signals? Have you met his family and friends? Are you his plus one when he attends weddings in his circle? Does he flirt with other women? Is he looking over your shoulder at a party? Why did his last three relationships fail? Hmmm . . . what is the pattern here?

This guy believes in marriage, and eventually will marry someone, but she may be the next woman after you or the third one—who knows? In his late thirties or early forties he may begin to understand that he can't have it all. A serial monogamist I know recently got engaged to be married. One of the last things he said to me before the big day was, "I hate to think I'm closing doors. There's so much out there!"

Really? "Well, at some point you have to close some doors to let other doors open," I said. I hope that marriage will help him grow up.

COMMITMENT PREDICTIONS

THE PLAYER

May keep five or so women on speed dial; seeks novelty with booty calls and lots of action. Does not call back the night after. Attracted to women sowing their wild oats. Will drop you from the rotation if you push for more time or attention.

COMMITMENT PREDICTION · Thinks no-penalty sex is the best thing ever invented and sees no reason to stop having fun. Hookups with this guy are guaranteed to go absolutely nowhere. Will keep dating for as long as possible, even as he gets older and the women get younger.

THE HAPPILY UNHITCHED

Feels no internalized pressure to commit; may appear to be lonely, while in fact he likes his status quo. Self-sufficient to a large degree, he resists being fixed up with dates. Likes to do things his way.

COMMITMENT PREDICTION · Needs a push, which an Alpha woman can do for him. A Beta woman, who might prolong the waiting, will need to activate her Alpha to start him up. In either case he needs a woman who is confident enough to be both firm and gentle, to take his hand and lead him to the altar. Don't be afraid of taking the initiative and seeing where it goes.

THE SERIAL MONOGAMIST

He's thinking long-term but his behavior is confusing. Takes his time as he looks for the perfect woman. Relationships stall at about six months in; envisions a traditional devoted woman who is also independent.

COMMITMENT PREDICTION · A woman has to rev up her Alpha and make decisions based on whether *she's* getting what *she* needs. The best fit for him is probably a strong Beta with Alpha tendencies who can prioritize him without pampering him.

RECOGNIZING THE QUINTESSENTIAL BETA MAN

Oliver, 31

    65 percent Beta, 40 percent Alpha

    High Beta/Mid Alpha

The most accurate way to separate Alpha from Beta bachelors is to connect the dots of their dating history. Once the pattern comes to light—aha!—you will be in a much better position to predict a person's future behavior. When you look at Oliver, you'll see that his relationship history is *progressive* (he isn't just repeating certain choices; he's learning and growing, making him a desirable Beta male).

Handsome but not drop-dead handsome, Oliver is a tech whiz who works for a start-up in business development. He has loads of pals to party with and close friends to confide in. He gets along with his parents, but lives alone and does not depend on them. Funny, smart, and down-to-earth, he values relationships and looks forward to marriage and a family. Oliver has chosen strong Alpha women whom he respects and admires. Each of his three serious monogamous relationships over the last ten years since college has lasted about one to three years.

Dating history
Relationship #1:

Oliver and his first girlfriend had a sweet romance that didn't develop into anything deeper. When she moved away, they visited each other, but after one and a half years, the relationship died a slow death by mutual consent. Eight years later, they are still friends and confidants. Oliver feels he can confide in her and seek advice about his romantic disappointments.

Relationship #2:

Cynthia, an Alpha woman who wanted more of a commitment than Oliver was ready for, brought a new level of seriousness to his life. Cynthia was confident that although they both prioritized their careers and were about to go to graduate schools in different cities, they should continue their exclusive relationship. She felt that they were so in love they should count on bringing their lives together in two years. After his first experience with a long-distance relationship, Oliver was unenthusiastic. He felt he was too young and too career focused to commit.

Cynthia tried to persuade him, and when that didn't work she pulled out all the stops with fits of anger and tears. He'd never realized how insecure and possessive she was. The more she pushed, the worse it was for Oliver, who hated confrontation and dreaded letting people down. In spite of this, he pushed back and stood his ground, with admirable care and sensitivity. He didn't want to hurt Cynthia, but he did not want to promise something he knew he couldn't deliver. After several months of drama, they separated and she unfriended him on Facebook. They have not spoken since.

Relationship #3:

Next up was Kerry, a woman who fit the bill in most respects but did not mesh with his strong values. Oliver met Kerry through a friend in business school. She was beautiful, smart, and sexy, and Oliver fell in love.

But Kerry had a big problem: an obsession with couture fashion that she could not afford—which had led, inevitably, to a bad credit card habit. Oliver, who is cautious and conservative about money, was appalled when he found out about her phenomenal debt. Even after she was laid off from her job, she kept shopping. She saw nothing wrong with how she was managing her life, but Oliver felt she was living in a bubble. He couldn't see how she'd ever pay off the debt—then understood she really had no intention of doing so. There was always a new collection that she had to see, new items she had to own. Barneys had her on speed dial, and her minutely organized closets held magnificent pickings from the chicest new designers. Her shoes had closets of their own. As the months went on, Oliver admitted to himself that Kerry was on a collision course and would soon need serious bailing out. Uneasy but still smitten, he gave her money to pay down one of her numerous cards.

But what would life be like with someone so obsessed and so irresponsible? Oliver knew that if the relationship were to continue, they'd have to talk. At dinner one night he got up his courage and introduced the subject of money and values. Could she imagine herself scaling down on her expenses? No, she said. A fashionable lifestyle meant more to her than anything else—and she couldn't imagine living any other way.

To her credit, Kerry had not fudged the truth, and now Oliver had to face facts—and he freaked out. How would this unfold if they got married? He still found Kerry beautiful and intriguing, but he did not want a life spent paying off her bills. Someday he wanted a family, and he couldn't imagine Kerry making any sacrifices.

After several more discussions over the next two months, the couple decided to part and sadly went their separate ways. Although Oliver thinks about her and misses her desperately, he said to a friend, with a combination of ruefulness and (mostly) relief, "I dodged a bullet."

Back on the dating scene, Oliver decided to try online even though he'd always resisted it because it was anonymous, and you never knew what you were getting. A twenty-seven-year-old woman texted him an invitation to come over, which he did. After fifteen minutes they had sex, and then never saw each other again. He was rather pleasantly shocked at himself. He'd just walked over, used a condom, and had great sex: his first experience with casual sex had gone well.

Now he wants a serious relationship—no playing around. He still prefers to meet people through friends. It feels weird to be dating people to whom he has no real-life attachment, so now he is using an algorithm to see what connections he can make between online dating and his friendships. In other ways, too, Oliver has the online dating scene down to a science. Well organized, businesslike, and highly motivated, he keeps notes and files on every woman he meets, so that there isn't any room for confusion.

After no more than three e-mails, he moves things along: If there is mutual interest, he initiates a phone call. If the conversation goes well, there might be one more call and then, without further ado, he schedules a meeting at a public place.

Oliver believes that anyone who stretches out the e-mail process is suspect, and I agree. Excessive e-mailing can have us legitimately asking, "What is the person hiding? Is there an agenda? Has he or she lied about age, height, or weight?" Cautiously, in anticipation of a possible bummer, he always makes the date for one hour *only*. ("I have another commitment at eight.") With experience, he is realistic that it might not pan out.

Oliver often schedules two encounters a night; at each one, he politely picks up the check and thanks the woman for her time. He usually follows up the next day with an e-mail or a text if he is interested. When one woman texted him to cancel at the last minute, he was going to call her and reschedule. I said, "No! She isn't reliable or considerate. Move on."

Oliver has a vision of a partnership in which he and his wife support each other and build a life together. He is hoping to get married within the next few years, and I am confident that he will find a strong Alpha woman he will cherish.

DON'TS FOR STRONG WOMEN

1. DON'T SETTLE

Dilemma: "I'm thirty-five. I feel like I'm dating with a gun to my head. Should I marry Mr. Right Now? He seems reliable and nice. What if I don't meet anyone as nice as he is? Is he my last chance?"

Advice: Don't panic. If you think Mr. Right Now is a possibility, give it a chance but don't settle. Tackle the online dating scene with greater focus and purpose. Pursue the activities you love with vigor and passion. Avoid the players. Consider divorced older men (in their forties).

Dilemma: "I'm thirty-one and I'm lonely. I've gone to six weddings in the last six months. Nothing has worked out for me. Should I lower the bar?"

Advice: Feeling sorry for yourself is not productive. It is the perfect time to start weeding out unavailable men. Weddings are a great place to meet guys. Don't lower your expectations, but prune them if they are unrealistic. There are plenty of guys out there, but you need to be smart and focused. You have time. Be positive!

Dilemma: "I'm pursuing a career that I love. My mom is getting nervous that I won't get married. But I'm too busy and I'm not in love with my boyfriend. Not only that, but at the age of twenty-seven, I don't want to get serious about anyone right now."

Advice: You have plenty of time. Your career is important for the long haul. If you want to marry, you should keep that clearly in mind in a year or two when you date. As for now, focus on your career.

Dilemma: "My boyfriend is steady and he's a great guy. But the chemistry has already died and we've only been seeing each other for a year. I'm thirty-eight. What should I do?"

Advice: Take a vacation. Buy some sex toys. Introduce novelty and adventure into your sexual relationship. Share your fantasies. Talk with your boyfriend about how to get lust back into your relationship. He sounds like a good guy who is worth investing in.

2. DON'T ENABLE

Dilemma: "I don't mind managing a lot of things at one time. Actually, I'm really good at it. I find that when I do things, they get done. My husband will do stuff, but it takes him forever and I get impatient. Sometimes I get exhausted. What should I do?"

Advice: Let him do things in his own way and in his own time. Don't be a control freak. Don't move in to do something just because you can do it. Manage your impatience. Let things slide a little; it will be good practice for you and be even better for your relationship. Above all, do not criticize the way he does things.

Dilemma: "A man I've started dating recently is warm and talkative—when he's alone with me. But when we meet friends for dinner, he shuts down to the point of rudeness, and I end up feeling as if I have to apologize for his behavior. It is embarrassing. What should I do?"

Advice: Don't be embarrassed and don't apologize for his behavior. He may feel overwhelmed by meeting your friends; it may bring out some shyness. Or he may be jealous of other people's claims on you. Talk this out. He may just need more time to get used to your friends.

3. DON'T TONE YOURSELF DOWN

Dilemma: "I'm really smart and I love to tell stories. I crave attention. But I've noticed that most men I go out with want to be the center of attention. I sit and make nice. Do I have to do that?"

Advice: You need a guy who appreciates your charm and can let you be center stage—at least some of the time. Your partner should not be looking for a wallflower, and he should be able to share the spotlight.

Dilemma: "I love parties of all kinds, and I always enjoy bantering and sparring with people. When things get slow, I stir the pot by making some challenging remark. My boyfriend gets nervous and tells me he doesn't like it when I go over-the-top. Is he right?"

Advice: Keep your observing ego tuned-in to your behavior. As long as you aren't being rude or inappropriate, then you're fine. At least no one will get bored when you're around!

CHAPTER 5

THE ALPHA AND BETA OF DATING

IN SOME WAYS ONLINE dating and social media have leveled the playing field; women can take charge of their dating and sex lives in ways they haven't before. Your Alpha penchant for taking risks is a plus, and in many ways the dating scene seems to have been made with you in mind. Women can initiate dates or group hangouts just as easily as men do. You can use the latest dating app and find someone new and attractive right around the corner. Sitting and waiting to be chosen looks pretty lame nowadays. The dating world revolves around proactive choices.

IS IT JUST SEX?

"A guy can put up an Instagram post that says 'I'm hungry,' with a picture of himself eating something," a woman in a focus group told me. "If someone sees it and feels in the mood, she can flirt back and hook up." A woman might make her own booty calls because she prefers to be in control. She doesn't like being just one among many on a guy's contact list. "I'm really stressed out, so this weekend, my plan is to have a lot of sex," she confides. She has some choices in mind.

What do women really think about casual sex? I asked a focus group to speak from their experiences:

- "You can have sex without consequences. Women can have sex and be totally detached."

- "I think it's definitely possible to enjoy casual sex, but if you make it a habit, it won't get you where you want to be in terms of a happy, long-term relationship."

- "I think women always think there should be something else, like a phone call the next day."

- "I believe anytime you hook up, you're going to establish some sort of connection; that's just basic human nature. Every individual woman will have a different way of dealing with that connection. I also don't think it's fair to say that men are immune to feeling those connections. Some women can have casual sex and be detached and some men can't have casual sex and be detached. It just depends."

- "Even hooking up with someone I know I wouldn't date, there are some emotions. It's the feeling of needing to be seen as the desired one."

- "When I know it's a one-night stand, casual sex can be totally fun, ego boosting, adventurous, and sexy. An Alpha guy can be pure sex. Like most of these men, I am an open, sexual person, and probably I am at the peak age of horniness!!"

- "A lot of women can have sex without the relationship part. But if it goes on for any amount of time, someone inevitably gets emotionally involved. It's just as easily the guy as the woman. Mike and I started out on the same page. We really liked each other, but it was supposed to be casual. He had more expectations than I did and he ended up getting hurt."

- "Even if I don't love this person or see potential for a serious relationship, it's almost impossible for me to have sex and then not feel something stronger for him. Whereas, I think men suppress their feelings and can focus on immediate satisfaction."

- "It's hard when you are single, horny, adventurous, and playful. It means you'll end up having lots of fun sex that'll always never be quite fulfilling, and it won't get you closer to your goal of finding a long-term partner. But, how else are you supposed to wait for your husband-to-be?"

- "I don't want to be husband hunting. I hate that idea. Still, I'm getting burned out from having relationships that don't pan out."

- "Sex will always have an emotional aspect to it. Hormones are released during close contact that stimulate feelings. With one guy I knew absolutely we weren't going to have a relationship. But for ten minutes after sex, I thought, *OK, I'm in love!* But that was straight-up hormones. When the ten minutes were over, it was, *Oh, shut up.* It had nothing to do with how I actually felt about him."

- "I was never into casual sex. I will have consistent sex with someone I like who I know I'm not going anywhere with. But I believe that sexually you do have to let a guy know what you expect. You have to decide what you want, like if going down is really important to me (and it is!), I wouldn't give him blow jobs if he wouldn't do that, though I'd be patient if he said give me some time. But a lot of guys really take pride in going down."

SHOP AROUND

As an observer and listener in the therapist's chair, I've seen us move into a postdating and postfeminist reality in which the old-fashioned date is just that—old. Men and women of all ages surf the dating sites and use social media. The dating sites report more than 593 million visits in the United States. It's a national pastime, no stigma attached! But of course there's an upside *and* a downside.

Along with the prolific opportunities for instantaneous contact, tech communications cause high anxiety. (It can give you a case of "relationship ADD," as one man put it.) The day of dating rules is over, and you can't fall back on assumptions from the past. I see my clients' frustration and confusion as they try to navigate the dating scene. People with ambiguous motivations are nothing new, but the cyberworld creates layers of obfuscation, and you have to be savvy to get an accurate read.

Over and over again, I listen to clients speaking of someone they think they know, simply because they've done Google searches, exchanged a lot of e-mails, Facebook posts, or texts—but it's a false assumption. It is important to remember that people may use their profiles as marketing tools to portray themselves as someone they wish to be—better or different from the real version. (In the extreme, a nonexistent "virtual self.")

At the same time you can shop around and maximize your options in a world that promises endless possibilities. A doctoral candidate in her midtwenties broke up with her boyfriend of two years, posted her profile online, and was inundated with replies. For her first date, she chose a man to meet for drinks, and for her second, a woman. "Why not?" she said. This is her time to experiment, explore her sexuality and identity, and figure out what she wants. After dating a succession of three men and breaking off from each of them—"they all wanted serious relationships, which I don't"—she's put dating on hold for the time being as she gets ready to leave for Africa to conduct research for her doctorate. A client of mine, already in a relationship, admitted to surfing the websites. She wasn't really interested in meeting anyone, she said, but since the marketplace serves up an endless supply of new people, why not see who is out there? You never know!

Scoring high on the Alpha end of the spectrum probably means that you can play the online dating game with less angst than someone with fewer Alpha qualities might. In a discussion, women and men in their mid to late twenties, all ambitious graduate students at a major university, are admittedly more interested in socializing and sex than long-term relationships right now. They agreed on a number of points. "Avoid a guy who writes too much about himself," advised one woman. "He's a narcissist." At the same time, when you write about yourself, "Don't be self-deprecating, twee, or too cutesy. Be a normal person, honest but not *too* honest." A man agreed: "Don't take yourself too seriously. That's a lost cause and seems pitiful. People should crack pithy little jokes; be funny, short and concise, and not sound *too* sincere." The group agreed that their least favorite self-description is the cop-out, "I don't know what to say about myself." This reveals the person to be inarticulate or unreflective—and a big turnoff.

Even if you aren't interested in anything serious, the group agreed that you should match on fundamental questions. Don't, for heaven's sake, go out with a creationist if you believe in evolution! Good grammar and spelling *do* matter (to this group). Finally, they said, forget the metacomments. Don't go on and on about how weird it is to be writing about yourself on a dating website. "Get over it," another man said. "You're doing it, everyone's doing it, and we're all here."

DATING ANGST

Once you're looking for something more serious, you need coping mechanisms, which will differ, depending on your personality, age, and the situation. A client named Kristen, twenty-nine, speaks with knowledgeable exasperation: "There's this whole cast of characters out there," she says. "It is so much work, and you go on lots of dates and nothing pans out. My friends and I stay upbeat about it, so we don't get discouraged. It can be pretty entertaining *if* you have the right attitude."

Kristen and her friends are looking for serious relationships. By sharing stories and frustrations, they give and get a sense of control. Together, they check off the boxes: "Like, I am looking for an athlete, someone Catholic," she says. "It helps me feel that if I keep shopping, I can get what I want. In my heart of hearts I don't really feel that I have much control. Some of the guys online are *really* weird. This friend of mine met a handsome guy who was an Ibanker [investment banker]. They hooked up once and after that he only communicated with her on Facebook, where everyone could see! It made her really uncomfortable."

These issues are universal, and cross generational, but with a different twist for different age groups. Kristen's mother, Jackie, is fifty-eight and divorced. She very much wants a partner, but she's disheartened. "My mom has had no luck in finding a companion," Kristen tells me. "She says there are so many creeps out there. I worry about her because I know she's lonely."

Younger people have cut their teeth on social media, so to them online dating may not seem like much of a stretch. But someone like Jackie feels as if she's learning a new language and new social customs. She feels uneasy about the whole notion of putting herself out there and communicating with strangers. Unfortunately, she may be more susceptible than the younger generations to the kinds of misrepresentation that people routinely engage in. She may get her hopes up too high and experience greater disappointments.

It may seem counterintuitive, but I'd advise Jackie, who is in a vulnerable position, to do the opposite of what the graduate students agreed on and make a strong, honest statement about her vision of life (her values and beliefs) and make it crystal clear what she wants in a partner and a relationship. One suggestion: search for a widower who already has a long-term relationship under his belt. Whether or not that appeals to her, she should cut straight to the chase, ditch the games, and sift through the inventory with a critical eye.

Jade, twenty-eight, said, "I had a really bad experience with a man who lost interest just as I was on the cusp of falling in love. I was really ready to take the plunge. It was horrible. I felt so much rejection and loss. Soon after that, two guys I knew asked me out. My therapist said, 'Why not see what happens if you go out with men who like you instead of those Alphas!' So I tried. I didn't like either of them. Now I feel as if I can't trust my own judgment."

Jade's therapist's suggestion was good, but the timing was off. Jade was still reeling from rejection and too vulnerable to take chances. At this point she will see men in a negative light. After she has healed from her disappointment, she will become more open again.

Her college friend, Tanya, said, "I want someone who is exciting and adventurous, not someone who has the right credentials, like my religion or social class. I want romance. But a lot of Alpha guys I'm meeting are empty inside. At the same time it sounds too easy just to say I have to find a supportive guy. I don't like guys who are over-accommodating. They're indecisive and insecure. I can't be with someone who doesn't go after what he wants."

Tanya is splitting men into categories: adventurous and exciting, supportive and indecisive or insecure. She understands that a lot of Alpha guys don't have much going on beneath the surface; at the same time she shouldn't feel she has to settle for a man with too many negative Beta qualities. She should hold out for the man who can be romantic and caring, and try to avoid splitting while she looks. Suffering hard knocks doesn't mean you won't find someone; it *does* mean learning from your mistakes, believing in yourself, and sticking to what you know you want.

THE OFF-AND-ON GAME

Beware the smartphone in the hands of a guy looking for casual sex: he's in his comfort zone when he's texting—playing a game of hide-and-seek that can have you tearing your hair out. Take this kind of date with a grain of salt; it could just be a flirt! This is quintessential Alpha male behavior, so don't personalize it. The ambiguous postdating environment can create the illusion of a connection without any real intimacy. People maintain these illusory connections with intermittent texts and serial hookups.

The operative word here is *intermittent*. Behavioral conditioning theory developed the concept of intermittent reinforcement: the more random and more unpredictable the reward, the more eagerly a subject responds. A thirty-seven-year-old physical therapist in private practice has an ongoing relationship that is based on intermittent texts and occasional dates. After not a peep from him for a couple of weeks, suddenly a text will pop up when she's getting ready to go to work, saying something like "94 degrees this AM. Keep cool!" He also canceled—by text—a New Year's Eve date the night before. She was a "train wreck," she says. Understandably, but the point is it's no surprise.

But she doesn't tell him how she feels. "I don't want to talk about it," she says. "I'm afraid of rejection. I'm guarded because I've been really burned before." She's being burned now, as this man is obviously not exclusive to her. "It is too upsetting to confront that," she tells me. But she is a smart, competent woman, and I suspect that she knows the truth.

Another attractive woman client, who recently decided she wanted a serious relationship, met a man online. They started texting, and his texts became flirtatious and seductive, as well as randomly timed, which kept my client in a state of anxious anticipation. In the four months after they met, she actually saw him only five times, and in four out of the five times they had sex. You can develop a ratio of how many flirty texts to live encounters to help you evaluate the true nature of a relationship. My intuition tells me that if the ratio is more than 4:1 in the early stages of dating, it's time to sign off.

FALSE POSITIVES

We all know the term: double message. This is when a verbal communication ("I am angry") is disqualified by a smile (I'm not *really* angry). The two messages, verbal and nonverbal, contradict each other, confusing the receiver. Double messages have been around forever, but now they are hidden in a new form, or medium, of communication.

Before technology, this was complicated; now it's even more so. Let's say it's 6:30 AM, and you get a text from a man you met at a party and hooked up with three days ago. This is the first time you've heard from him since then. The content of this text ("I'm thinking about you") and the timing (who says this at the crack of dawn, maybe your mother) is intimate and in direct contrast to the metacommunication, which refers to the method of his message (here, casual texting). He catches you off guard, and you're not sure how to respond.

What's odd is that the message *suggests* more intimacy than is real. He is throwing out a feeler in a safe context. Don't take it as genuine interest. It is only a flirtation. I call this the false positive in the dating game. Timing is key: if you text back immediately, your response tells him that you're willing to participate in a casual relationship. If that is what you want, fine. But if a casual relationship is not for you, you need to let a few days pass before you answer (if you actually are interested in pushing things up a notch). Then you will be signaling *some* interest while discouraging the false intimacy of an early-morning text. The time frame of your reply actually reveals *more* than words do. Am I advocating game playing? No. But cybercommunication is just as complicated, if not more so, than verbal, and you need to be fluent in the language.

Beware the overly casual communication. Someone you've seen a few times will text, "Let's try to make it next Wednesday." When Wednesday rolls around, you text *him* around 5:00 PM, and he says he has to work. Beware of any sentence that begins: "let's try . . ." It sounds friendly, but it promises nothing.

If you score high on the Alpha graph, you are probably used to being in control—and may end up surprisingly vulnerable in the dating game. "Alphas do better in business than they do with men," one woman told me. "In relationships, you have to worry about feelings; in business you don't." Even though you genuinely enjoy your sexual nature and your hot encounters with macho guys, you may be afraid that if you allow yourself to reveal your deeper feelings and desires, you'll be hurt. It's intimacy that makes things dicey for you.

As an Alpha, you will need to manage certain qualities, namely your impulsivity and your need for control. Let's say that you're online, looking for a relationship. When you meet someone who intrigues you, you get to work, trying to seduce him right away with clever texts. The trouble is he doesn't get a chance to breathe (as one man succinctly put it). As an Alpha, you would like to take charge of the dating experience as much and as soon as possible. The problem is that although you *can* be proactive, you *can't* control the process as much as you would like and firmly believe you can.

You may tend to pursue men who are challenging, because you're convinced that you can *make* something happen. You're a powerful person, after all! Texting is so easy that it may enable your tendency to pursue too hard. One of my Alphas barrages new prospects with texts, which usually, no surprise, tends to make guys feel harassed. This is a big mistake. Big. It may *seem* safe to assume that an easy, casual mode of communication will disguise your eagerness and, as a bonus, show off how smart you are. But while a series of quick hellos and witty remarks may seem harmless, it actually may convey overeagerness or, worse, desperation. To be blunt, at the beginning you don't know if someone is just playing with you. Technology teaches us that everything is instantaneous, like magic, so we have to teach ourselves that developing a relationship is not. It will take several dates to psych *anyone* out.

"LET ME SOLVE YOUR PROBLEMS"

Some Alpha women are suckers for guys with problems. Confident, determined, and terrific problem solvers, they like to take a guy on and make him all better. What a great project for a high-energy woman!

A successful advertising salesperson, Laura began her career late but rose rapidly. Well suited to her profession, she is warm, sociable, attractive, and not in the least bit shy. She has tons of friends who adore her, loves throwing extravagant parties, is knowledgeable about art, and enjoys the cultural scene of New York City. Since her divorce seven years ago, she's been meeting men on- and offline—and having absolutely no success. Given how very appealing Laura is, this is a puzzle—until you realize that she either chooses rejecting Masters of the Universe (her first husband) or the opposite, Omega losers.

The daughter of a critical mother, Laura is used to being the brunt of mean remarks. The first remark a recent date made was, "Boy, that picture in your profile must be really old." The photo was recent, and Laura looked great! His remark stung, but she laughed it off and spent the next two hours listening to him talk and giving advice. If a man makes a critical or insulting comment on a first date, he is testing how much rejection and manipulation you'll tolerate. At best he has a mean streak; at worst, he may be an abuser. Turn right around and leave.

And then there are the losers. Laura and a date spent ten hours in Central Park in the spring, wandering among the green meadows, flowering cherry trees and gardens, passing one inviting, private bench after another. "Why in the world can't we sit down and make out?" Laura wondered, fantasizing about what it would be like to kiss this attractive man. Instead they kept walking and talking—but not touching, not even holding hands. After they parted ways at the end of the day, he texted her to say what a nice day he'd had. Laura, frustrated to the point of bursting, fired a text right back: "I really wish we'd kissed. I'm a very good kisser." His reply? "I have issues."

Issues? I was not surprised. Any man who walks around the park for several hours with you and doesn't even hold your hand? Well, what can I say? Of course he has issues. I asked her, "How did you respond?" She told him that they should make a date and talk about his problems. She was genuinely curious, but in this case, Laura's curiosity and empathy were misplaced. Generally, you should resist a discussion of issues in the first stages of a relationship. You do not want to be a man's therapist; you want a lover and a friend. And to have fun! Let him figure out his issues and then give you a call. Being a fixer is not sexy or romantic; it's more like signing up to be a wet nurse to a baby. Is this really what you want?

Guys in need of help were not new for Laura. Her first engagement, many years before, had ended when her fiancé, who avoided sex with her throughout their engagement, finally admitted he was gay. In this case why try to "fix something that ain't broke?" Her fiancé's only issue was that he was attracted to men.

Laura is Alpha at work and with her friends, but her secret is that with men her Alpha ("I can solve your problems") works against her. She thinks she is taking charge, but, in reality, she is letting the man lead—and letting him hurt her. Because she is resilient and tough, she manages the hurt by shrugging it off. A great storyteller, she gives each disappointing encounter a name (the guy in Central Park was Elvis because he was a rock musician) and adds another hilarious item to her tales of dating woe. She is a natural entertainer—but at a great cost.

Laura is on a roller coaster of hope and dismay. Dating gives her an adrenaline rush, and she fuels it with a lot of bubbling energy. One of the Alpha's biggest problems is that she is drawn to super-Alpha guys like a moth to a flame. She likes the challenge of getting what she believes is the prize: the sexiest, most exciting, challenging cowboy out there. She can make it happen! But at the same time she needs to move beyond the choices she's made until now and focus on finding a strong Beta man who can be a respectful, independent partner. He will allow her to take the lead and desire her sexually (no issues permitted). The best way for Laura to start is to size up the situation quickly, eliminate anyone who seems the least bit rejecting, and move on. And even though Laura loves a good story, she shouldn't let that get in her way. Finding a good relationship will make the best story of all.

WHAT GAME PLAYING SAYS ABOUT YOU

The whole notion of gender differences as opposed to gender similarities has led us to believe, among other things, that men are ambivalent about relationships while women are not. It's a self-fulfilling prophecy: men are taught that they're ambivalent, so they believe it and so do women. However, ambivalence about intimacy is a human trait, not a gender trait.

Thirty-year-old Blair *thought* she wanted a relationship, and when she met a man online whom she liked, became very excited and hopeful. They exchanged rounds of texts. And more texts. They were going in circles, flirting and chitchatting, hiding-and-seeking. In a session she and I realized it was a game; partly she was eager to meet someone, and partly, she was quite scared. Coming off some bad relationships, she was ambivalent and used endless texting as a stalling tactic.

Participants in a small study about texting and relationships said that texting can work in the early stages as a way to establish a connection and ease social anxiety, but that face-to-face interaction must soon follow. Texting is a safe, but nonintimate form of communication that can be used by both women and men in a self-protective, avoidant way. If you find yourself in an endless texting situation similar to Blair's, you need to take stock. Ask yourself: Why am I stalling? What am I afraid of? Being comfortable with your fear and plunging in anyway will help you master whatever it is that you are afraid of. The typical fears of exposure and rejection will be more manageable as you gain experience in relationship building.

If you're genuinely interested in someone, you need to push yourself to take it to the level of face-to-face communication—guaranteed to be the only way you will be able to tell who this person really is and what he wants. Keep some control by exchanging three or four e-mails or texts, and then, if you feel like taking a shot, meet the guy. It always takes time to get to know someone, so you might as well get started. Who has time to waste?

The potential for gaming in the cyberhookup culture is endless and varied, and many Alpha women enjoy it. Hannah, an anthropology doctoral candidate in her midtwenties, hooked up with a guy she thought was cute. She wasn't too sure how she felt about him, but she wondered if he'd text her the next day. If he did, he'd be "saying" that he really liked her. Instead he friended her on Facebook. She decided he was being cagy and trying to let her down easy. Finally, three days after the hookup, he texted her, the correct etiquette for contacting someone you've had a hookup with, but aren't all that interested in. When Hannah and her friends realized the text arrived at *exactly* seventy-two hours posthookup, they took control of the message by mocking his meticulous attention to form.

The fact is both Hannah and the guy had been counting down the hours and minutes after the hookup, jostling for the psychological upper hand as they determined the outcome of their encounter. Hannah didn't want to feel rejected or acknowledge her disappointment; she was coming out of a difficult two-year relationship, so with the support of her friends, she made a game out of interpreting the meaning of his communications. She was in it as much as he was, but gaming it gave her emotional distance from the experience. I kept it to myself, but I thought, "This hypervigilance is a constructive form of self-protection." Hannah clearly was determined not to dwell on the hookup, and that was healthy.

Game playing can really be taken to ridiculous heights (or depths).

This tale of monstrous deception may sound like a bad dream, but I assure you it's all too real. Suspicious that his girlfriend Lisa was dating other guys, Geoffrey masterminded a plan to smoke her out. One night, as they were lying in bed after sex, he created a false online identity on Match.com that he knew would intrigue her. Within the next hour, while both were on their iPhones, Lisa sent an e-mail response to his posting. With her lying next to him in bed, Geoffrey asked for her photo, which she *immediately* sent. Then, as if nothing had happened, they turned out the lights and went to sleep.

That was just the beginning. The next day, he accused her of "betrayal and disloyalty," claiming that the post on Match belonged to a friend of his, who'd told him that she'd responded to it. Worse, he said, since everyone in his circle knew he was dating her, she had humiliated him. Having been outed, Lisa was horrified. She'd had, she insisted, no intention of meeting the other man.

Later, she got a funny feeling about the whole thing. She knew Geoffrey well enough to know that he was a schemer. She'd been set up—no doubt about it. She accused *him* of betrayal, which led to his accusing her of the same, which led to accusations that continued for weeks. They were both right: neither was trustworthy, and since trust is the foundation of a real relationship, neither is available for true intimacy and love. My guess about these two? I think they will end up back together. After all, they are a perfect match in their capacity for deceit.

NO MORE SELF-BLAME FOR BETAS

If you skew more Beta than Alpha, you may really dislike game playing; you'd never find yourself in a cutthroat Lisa-and-Geoffrey situation. In fact, you'd rather die. You're not dating for the adrenaline rush; you're dating because you actually want to find a relationship.

In that way, you're usually more straightforward than an Alpha. Your problem may be that you invest yourself emotionally too soon or worry more about other people's feelings than you do about your own. If something doesn't work out, you get right to work blaming yourself. "What did I do wrong?" you wonder, mentally scrutinizing your long list of self-perceived faults.

One single mother, who had very little time to waste, would date men she met online and find herself chitchatting away long after she knew she wasn't interested. She was too nice to get up and leave! "I'd find myself stuck listening to some guy's tale of woe," she says. "His ex-wife said this or did that, and on and on. I'm a good listener and people like to talk to me; I know this about myself. But I'd end up giving advice as if I were his therapist or his mother." In this case, my strong suggestion is to activate your Alpha and practice politely ending things quickly. Check your watch and say, "Oh, I'm sorry, but I have to go. I lost track of time. It was very nice to meet you," and be on your way. It's entirely possible to incorporate this behavior even if you've never thought of yourself as Alpha. "I'm much better now," the single mom said. "I give it fifteen minutes as I assess my feelings. Is there basic chemistry? Is he interesting? Does he laugh at my jokes? Is he giving anything back to me, or is this conversation all about him? If the answer is no, no, no, no, I bring the meeting to an end."

Many Betas—although it's a question of the *degree* of Beta—are at risk of hanging in too long with ambivalent men. They may fear rocking the boat, avoid confrontation, and be way too willing to cede power. If you're trying too hard, like Laura, ask yourself why you choose men who are rejecting. What are you getting out of this? Ask: does he see this relationship as long-term? If you're in your thirties, and know you want marriage and children, you need to know by the end of the first year into a relationship what to expect. Hope is not a plan for the future.

Over a period of five years, Caroline, who is high Beta/mid Alpha, dated Steven, broke up with him, got back together, and allowed him to move in with her, hoping that marriage, which she knew she wanted, was on the horizon. When they first met, they quickly became close, but there were early signs that a relationship would not be a shoo-in. Because of their religious differences and his fear of parental disapproval, Steven resisted introducing Caroline to his family, and during the holiday season he went home alone to Wisconsin. As years two and three passed, they shared more and more, but Steven continued to avoid acknowledging their intimacy with a commitment to marriage.

Caroline, thirty-two, hates confrontations and ultimatums. Raised to be polite, accommodating, and charming, she is well educated and accomplished in her career. But Caroline's inner reality does not match up with appearances.

As the horizon of their relationship stretched out endlessly and the fifth year of the relationship loomed, Caroline's protective older brother, Edward, spoke up, admitting his concern that she had trapped herself with a man who had some deep-seated resistance to marriage. Unmarried himself, Edward thought he could identify a fellow commitmentphobe. Caroline didn't tell her brother that she feared pushing Steven too hard. Whenever she mentioned marriage, Steven became upset and said he needed more time. So Caroline backed away, far too willing to put his indecisiveness ahead of her personal goals.

Edward encouraged Caroline to give Steven a deadline, but she refused. She believed that Steven loved her, and she felt she could read his intentions and believed he'd come through. But Edward, who was accustomed to taking the lead with Caroline, kept pushing her to set a date for his decision, and finally she did. But when the date arrived, she and Steven pushed it back. After this happened four or five times, the dates to make a decision became meaningless.

The clues to her behavior lie in her childhood. Growing up, Caroline was overshadowed by Edward, the star of the family, and her self-esteem had suffered. By putting Steven's fears ahead of her need for a stable future, Caroline was repeating the family pattern in which her brother was placed on a pedestal and she looked up. As an adult, she devalued her own needs in order to please men. By cutting Steven so much slack, she fed into his indecisiveness and immaturity.

Now Caroline's biological clock was ticking insistently. She was entirely justified in wanting an answer. Ultimatums sound harsh but if you love a man and believe he loves you, you can give him a push to stand up and be counted. Don't allow his ambivalence to color your reality, and certainly don't let yourself be degraded and humiliated by his ambivalence. So, even though she had already lost credibility by moving her deadline so many times, I encouraged Caroline to try again—and this time make it stick.

PRIMA DONNA PLUS

Alpha women are usually determined to get *exactly* what they want, and sometimes they devalue people who are not as successful or self-confident as they are. Or they have a diva fantasy of a man who does everything just as they want him to or a wish for the perfect mate. If you keep expecting to meet a Master of the Universe who is also caring and supportive and sensitive, you may wait forever.

But let's distinguish between settling for less than you want and deserve and being an imperious diva and never taking no for an answer. "Maybe I should settle and marry him," a thirtysomething woman will sigh. I can't say how many times I hear this from women frustrated in their search for a partner and pressured by time. My response is always the same: never settle! Making a huge compromise when you choose a life partner is not a workable solution. Don't even think about settling as a viable option.

Then again, I have a super-Alpha client named Ashley who is dating a really nice Beta guy named Chris. She insists that he do things her way: dress in a certain style, give up his motorcycle, and, lately, stop seeing his best friend because she resents the time they spend together. If he won't do it, she says, it's a deal breaker. Ashley's dream is of a cocoon-like existence where she is in complete control.

This is narcissistic behavior to a T. She feels entitled and impressed with her own importance; at the same time, her unreasonable demands show how vulnerable and insecure she is. A secure person isn't threatened by a partner having an independent life. I have watched as she's pushed Chris into a corner, increasing her demands until he will be forced either to give her up or give himself up. This relationship will only survive if she can hold up a mirror to herself and see that her constant refrain is "my way or the highway."

Real people and real relationships rarely match up to our fondest fantasies. Ashley has a man who respects and loves her, but she wants to control his every move. I've seen other Alphas, and Betas as well, get in their own way when they persist in holding on to fantasies instead of getting to know the guy who shows them affection and respect. Keep in mind that the most important characteristic of a successful marriage is something called a vision of life. Shared beliefs and values and similar ideas about family make up the *core* of a marriage that works. Throw in good sex, and you have a recipe that will serve you well over the long haul. Granted, there's a fine line between settling and being realistic. But try to think less about a guy's imperfections and more about the qualities that match up to your vision of life (which should include, it goes without saying, good, although not necessarily mind-blowing-all-the-time sex).

Remember, the marriage statistics are way in your favor: so, expand your search, put your fantasies aside, and take a real-life risk.

CHAPTER 6

BECOMING A COUPLE

I WAS RAISED IN a generation of women who were defined by marriage. Adult status was conferred with a marriage certificate, and no one questioned the wisdom of that. At one time an unmarried woman was considered a wizened old spinster by her late twenties. She was caricatured as pitiful, living alone with a clowder of cats. While the cultural pressure isn't quite that bad today, it is still bad enough. It's as if, after thirty, a woman starts closing in on her expiration date.

Courtship used to be focused on getting a woman married as soon as possible. Someone asked you out, and if you liked each other, you dated some more, until finally, with enough mutual interest and a modest degree of commitment, you had sex, which launched a "real" relationship that probably led to marriage.

Today, the single adult woman has many things on her agenda besides marriage. Molly, twenty-nine, has been dating the same man for four years. Busy and involved at work, she isn't rushing to the altar. But her co-workers, including people whom she manages, nag her about when she's going to set the date. She shrugs it off as intrusive and annoying. Molly has her own timetable for marriage. Like many people, she is choosing to stay single longer. She's not waiting for him to "put a ring on it" to become an official adult.

Carolyn, also in her twenties, is a busy journalist with an active, popular blog. She admits she sometimes "worries about how comfortable I am without a man. I just call my girls and we go out and have a great time! I think about planning a single life in case I don't meet someone I really like." At this point Carolyn does not see singledom as a tragedy—far from it. Her primary worry is that when she gets old, "Who will do for me what I do for my parents?" Her friend answered this for her: "You'll live in a community of people so someone can wheel you to the store if you need help!"

A 2013 study from Pew Research revealed that 27 percent of respondents were unsure of whether they wanted to marry. This ambivalence about the married state may be linked with the seeming fragility of the institution in the decades since the 1970s, as divorce became more common (although not as common as we've been led to believe). Still, many men and women who are in their twenties and thirties grew up with their parents' divorce, or saw it played out in friends' families and in the media—and it does have an effect. Psychologist Judith Wallerstein's landmark study of the grown children of divorce found that many are leery of commitment and may prefer to cohabitate rather than to marry. In fact, for a number of reasons, cohabitation rates have been rising for decades. (According to the US Census Bureau, the rate of cohabitation has risen from 450,000 couples in 1960 to 7.5 million in 2012.)

But the notorious one-in-two statistic (one in two marriages ends in divorce) you've heard so much about is misleading; since 1980, the divorce rate for college-educated women has actually significantly dropped, creating an economic "divorce divide," according to a study at the University of Maryland. And although 39 percent of Americans say they agree that marriage is becoming obsolete, most people who have never married say that they would like to marry someday (including many who agree that marriage is becoming obsolete). According to federal data, at least 80 percent of Americans will marry at some point in their lives.

I know from my practice that people's lives follow many roads, and a great deal has changed, but that marriage is still the gold standard for most people. In a focus group of seven college-educated women in their twenties, one woman was married, two were in serious relationships (one in a live-in arrangement with an agreement to become engaged within the year, and the other living-apart-together, or LAT), while four were looking for serious relationships. Every woman in the room raised her hand when I asked how many wanted to get married.

WHAT A RELATIONSHIP IS *NOT*

How can you tell if you are building a solid partnership? Without adhering to some ladder of commitment, relationships are amorphous and can be misleading, so here is a guide to what may seem like a complicated board game.

Let's start with a list of what is *not* a budding relationship:

1. He is on your booty-call list, and you've had some great hookups. You know it, but I will remind you again: Booty calls and hookups are about sex and convenience. Booty calls beget booty calls. They hardly ever convert—even if you lounge around comfortably after sex and think you've made a connection.

2. He sends lots of flirty texts and/or e-mails, followed by—nothing. The ratio of texts to face-to-face communication has to favor face-

to-face: maybe at most 4:1 (texts to in-person communication). Texts are way too easy. Actual dating requires such things as eating together, taking a walk, and seeing a movie.

3. He's rarely around, physically or virtually. You saw him a month ago, and after you text him several times, he finally replies three weeks later. This is a casual relationship that holds little promise.

4. He is a last-minute date breaker. Don't give him a second chance unless you know for sure that he has a demanding boss who lords it over him. Breaking a date means something better came up. Delete his contact information.

5. He often says, "Let's play it by ear," and resists making plans.

WHAT A RELATIONSHIP *IS*

I tell clients to think of relationships in terms of levels of commitment, which don't necessarily fall into the neatest of categories. I'll start with a caveat about hookups. Does a hookup *ever* convert into a relationship? Only if the hookup isn't exactly . . . a hookup. Felicity and Rick met at a party. She was very attracted to him, and they went back to her house. "At first I thought it was a hookup," she admits. "That was OK with me. But we had three hours of conversational foreplay. We talked about everything before we had sex." The next morning, Rick took the initiative by asking her to have dinner that night—and the relationship was off and running. Now they are living together and plan to get engaged within a year. Felicity smiles as she says, "If I had followed my religious upbringing, I would never have hooked up, and this never would have happened. What made it different was that we talked and we both knew that this was something different for both of us."

LEVEL ONE: SEEING EACH OTHER, HANGING OUT, HAVING SEX

You've met, and you're spending time together. Either of you can initiate, but you make a plan together. You show up. He shows up. You might sit around your apartment, take a hike, go to dinner, see a movie, bike, or meet friends. You like each other. Some women have sex by the second or third date. Others wait until things are further along. After that, if you are interested in a monogamous relationship and don't like the idea of being on anyone's rotation, you will want to have a conversation so that both of you are clear.

If you agree just to see each other, good. You move along toward greater intimacy. You communicate. You make eye contact. You tell jokes. You discuss things that interest you. If this is happening with some frequency, you are solidly on level one. Bravo! However, if it continues in this impromptu fashion for three months or more, don't count on its going any further.

PS: An Alpha woman may push her agenda too soon. She likes him and assumes that because she wants him to be on board he will be. You will need to listen and avoid getting impatient. Time will tell.

LEVEL TWO: GETTING TO KNOW EACH OTHER

This stage involves the steadiness and frequency of your dating pattern. If you see each other sporadically or infrequently, you are *not* here. (Go back to level one.)

In level two, even if you don't know exactly when you're going to see each other, you know you will. You can count on that. Your dates are frequent (at least once, more likely two or three times a week). Weekends are for sure. You may make casual plans: Come over and hang out. Let's have brunch on Sunday. Call when you're finished working and we'll grab a bite.

Since this is more serious dating, it can result in relationship claustrophobia, and one of you may feel that you need space. Are you ignoring each other's texts? Do either of you break plans at the last minute? Are you unsure of what he is doing on Saturday night? Is he unsure of what *you're* doing? Things may be going too fast. You may be uncertain about your feelings, or one or both of you has a problem with intimacy, even to a small degree. Pay attention.

Once you've dated someone for three to six months, you need to zero in on where the relationship is going. By now, you know you like him, and basically you want to know if he wants what you want. Is he interested in dating other people at this point? Would he like the two of you to spend more time together? I have found that most women have a problem at this stage. Some Alphas pretend that they're cool with an ongoing level one dynamic. One woman in her late twenties, who runs her own successful coffee shop business, is afraid to ask the guy she dates for what she really wants: more time together. She says, "Sexually, I have no trouble being assertive. I don't feel emotionally vulnerable in bed. It's asking for other stuff that scares me—like hanging out on Saturday."

With her friends she analyzes his behavior: What did he mean when he said that? And what about this? She's afraid to ask him, because he might say something she doesn't want to hear. Instead she keeps fantasizing and hoping. But isn't it better to know? True, you may not want to hear what he says. But brace yourself and gather up that Alpha ballsiness and put it out there. You need to know where things stand.

Meanwhile, Betas, who are good communicators once they get going, need to be aware of their inclination to be indirect, which can lead to misunderstandings that will frustrate you both. Don't circle around the topic and hope he gets it; be blunt even if it is uncomfortable. Remember, you are establishing a pattern of relating and you don't want to be a silent partner.

The best reply you can get from a man you like at this level would go something like this: "I really like you, and I want to spend more time together and get to know you better."

LEVEL THREE: BASIC COUPLEDOM

You are monogamous; you have both taken yourselves off the dating sites. You see each other as much as possible, definitely on weekends, and have good sex and personal conversations. As you get to know each other, occasional disagreements arise. He forgets to call after you gave the big presentation you told him about. You get annoyed when he doesn't clean up after you made dinner. You/he are on your phones when you are out to dinner. (This one is bad!)

You are starting to know each other's friends. You are his significant other at his friends' weddings. You might be meeting each other's parents if they are in town. You know more about each other and can trust sharing personal information that is not so rosy: perhaps you are intimidated by your boss, fear losing your job, or have a brother/sister/mother/father with a serious problem or illness.

You lead your separate lives, but you do not make plans for the weekend without first consulting each other. You talk or text every day, probably several times a day. You know what is going on in each other's lives and offer support and advice. You are relaxed around each other and realize how comforting intimacy is. Your sex is good, maybe even getting better as you share more of your sexual fantasies. Together, you research travel ideas, and you are both enthusiastic about planning your first vacation together.

LEVEL FOUR: COHABITATION

The plot thickens. If you decide to live together, treat it as a move that merits candid discussion and consideration. Sharing space for convenience—your apartment lease is expiring so you might as well combine forces—is a bad idea. "Might as well" is not good enough. Ask each other: Why exactly are we making this move? Is it for convenience or to save money? Is marriage on the horizon? Make sure you're on the same page.

A client of mine named Mitchell almost got himself into hot water when his long-distance girlfriend Dana said she wanted to move in with him when she came back East for a summer internship. He'd been having serious reservations about the relationship, but agreed to her moving in anyway. Then he found himself in an awful dilemma. He didn't want the move to happen, but wasn't emotionally prepared to break up either. As the move-in date approached and his anxiety rose, he initiated conversations about why their relationship didn't work. They eventually agreed to break up. Mitchell is a nice Beta guy. Some Alphas would have thought nothing of it, but that isn't him.

Cohabitation is serious—maybe not quite as much as marriage, but if you break up, it'll be almost as messy and painful as a real divorce. It's like playing house, with consequences. Sometimes people collude in a decision to live together because they share in a myth of commitment. They can be sort of married and keep the whole issue on the back burner. Or they actually have polar-opposite agendas: one person sees living together as a convenience, while the other assumes that it's a step toward engagement and marriage. This misunderstanding will eventually blow up in your face.

Two years before marriage, Yvette and Roger, both in their late twenties, moved in together. "Living together was a necessity for us before we could agree to marry," Yvette says. From the day they met in 2006 until 2009, the couple had a long-distance relationship. "Living together definitely helped us," she adds. "But it wasn't a perfectly blissful process."

From a young age, Roger had been fiercely independent and worked hard for a steady paycheck. Moving in coincided with his decision to quit work to attend design school full-time, so that he could eventually go out on his own as an entrepreneur. Yvette volunteered to shoulder their shared expenses. She says, "I was happy to do it, because I was moving upward financially, and I could comfortably afford it. But even though Roger has always been avidly supportive and proud of my success, relying on me financially was a major adjustment. I'm not sure he ever got fully comfortable with it."

Before long, tensions were escalating. "As his breadwinning girlfriend who also happens to be an Alpha woman," Yvette says, "I know that I often took it upon myself to make executive decisions about things like how often or whether to have a cleaning lady, whether or not to redecorate, and household finances. I probably should have involved him, and I know I wasn't always fair, but I held the purse strings. I had to learn to incorporate him into decisions that affected both of us—and that was a huge adjustment for me."

The whole experience of living together was a period of adjustment and compromise for both partners. Yvette says, "I travel a lot for work, which I can't compromise on right now unfortunately. Also, I don't cook, and I prefer to hire out things like cleaning and ironing that take away from my personal time. This somewhat shattered Roger's very conventional expectations of living with a girlfriend/fiancée/wife who does womanly things. Compromising hasn't been easy for either of us."

The couple went into their two-year cohabitation test drive with a basic sense that things would work out for them. "It was a risk, but I always knew Roger wanted to be married eventually," Yvette says.

"He's old-fashioned in that way." Still, they decided to do nearly a year of premarital counseling before getting married to sort out some trust issues that Roger had. "The counseling was a painful, extraordinarily humbling experience," she says. "It helped us in ways that even living together could not."

Looking back on their marriage of two years, Yvette says, "I work in banking and before I met Roger, I was really attracted to Alpha males. But they were the mirror image of me, and I could see they were incredibly self-absorbed. I knew I needed someone who complements me and knows what I like and what's important to me. I love Roger, and he loves me more than anyone ever did. He is amazingly thoughtful and considerate and sexy. We make each other feel complete."

For Yvette, cohabitation was a carefully planned move. She assessed the risk before making the decision and felt that the odds were in her favor. But many Alpha and Beta women alike make the mistake of assuming that cohabitation will lead to marriage. Men are more prone to see it as an arrangement on a trial basis or as a way to circle around making a commitment. Before anyone shows up with suitcases, a cat, or a sofa, please be sure to have a precohabitation discussion so that you're clear about motivations and goals and expectations. Otherwise, as psychologist Meg Jay points out, couples who live together operate on the principle of "sliding, not deciding": as couples slide from one stage to the next—dating to sleeping over to living together—they may skip not only rings and bouquets but, more important, truthful, realistic discussions about goals and expectations.

This was what happened to Amy. After law school in Boston, she planned to move back to her hometown, New York City, for her first job as an attorney. Her boyfriend, Max, lived in an apartment in Brooklyn, so the question was whether she should move in with him or get her own place. Amy thought they should live together; after all, they'd been dating seriously for about six months. Also, she had a demanding new job, and cohabitating would make things easier.

Amy was madly in love, and she assumed that Max was, too. They were sexually compatible; they were both athletic and loved outdoor activities, and they'd merged their friendship circles. Everyone they knew considered them a real couple. Neither had any interest in seeing anyone else, and Amy was sure that someday they'd marry and have children. In her mind, they were at least halfway to the altar.

After they'd been happily living together for a while, Amy casually raised the issue of getting engaged. She figured this was a no-brainer. Always a straight shooter, Max gently told her that he wasn't ready. For him, it was way too early to tell; marriage was a huge decision and they were just getting to know each other and enjoying their relationship. So why rush things? Amy was shocked and confused to find that although marriage was on her horizon it wasn't on his.

This couple made a common mistake by not discussing their expectations and what it meant to move in together. This is a perfect example of two people out of sync in their ideas and in their pacing.

As they tried to talk their conflict through, tension escalated until Max finally admitted that he wasn't sure they were well matched for the long haul. This was even worse than Amy had thought. "After all this time?" she gasped. "In what way?" Again, in a gentle but honest way he told her that she was not the partner he envisioned for himself. "Tell me what you mean," she pressed him.

"I need someone to challenge me," he said. "You're too agreeable."

Too agreeable! Stung, Amy was silent. As a strong Beta woman, she knew she tended to be accommodating and that she disliked confrontation. I can't change that about myself, she thought, devastated to realize that he was disappointed in her. Worse, she'd been blindsided by his confessions. After more tearful discussions and soul-searching, Amy broke off the relationship and moved in with a friend.

As Amy and I talked, she realized that Max was not someone who could be pushed into doing anything before he was ready. This shows his integrity; plus, he'd been honest and truthful with her. Finally, Amy decided that even though she still loved him, she had to start dating again and try to get over him. After making her decision, she cried herself to sleep for many nights, but I believed that she was a resilient young woman who would bounce back. In a few weeks, she went on Match and started dating.

Out of the blue, a few months later, Max called. He missed her, and he wanted to try again. I felt she needed to be very clear, and I told her, "You can't turn yourself into a pretzel to please someone else. You aren't ever going to be the sort of challenging person who is in his face. You have great qualities that he really should appreciate, like your sensitivity, social ease, and sense of humor. Max needs to love you for who you are."

Ultimately, I think Max respected Amy for being true to herself. She was not a confrontational person, but she was not so accommodating as to misrepresent herself or to try to change her basic personality to please him.

Amy and Max decided to give the relationship another chance. Their deal was that either could walk away, and they were not going to live together until Amy had a ring on her finger. Over the course of the next few months, the couple built their relationship on a new mutual understanding and respect for each other.

In this case, a crisis over cohabitation actually led to a couple communicating their true needs and goals. Amy and Max have been married for a few years now. He became less critical and more accepting (good Beta qualities for a purely Alpha guy!) and truly values her gentle, sensitive approach. She, never a pushover, became much less shy about making her needs known (a healthy Alpha attitude for an essentially Beta woman).

Having an understanding before moving in together can save you a lot of pain and confusion down the road. Cohabitating is not official on anyone's books, but for your own sake you have to be sure you're on the same page.

Sometimes couples want to stop at cohabitation. People have many reasons why they decide against official marriage. Again, you both need to understand your particular reasons. Miranda and Larry, in their late twenties, have been a couple since middle school and have been living together for a decade. Miranda sees no reason to marry. "I don't think marriage is the answer for us," she says. "Politically, I don't want to be forced to define who 'my people' are. We should be able to do what we want without marriage." At the same time, for all intents and purposes, she is married. She just hasn't made it legal.

Miranda, with fairly even amounts of Alpha and Beta, is determined to do things her own way. The younger of two sisters, she saw her own controlling, stay-at-home mother focus her life on her children. "She was really interfering," Miranda says. "Her children were her work and her hobby. She wished she had another kid after me. My parents' marriage is a mystery to me; they don't go anywhere or do anything together." Miranda says that her mother is a hypochondriac—and fears that she is deeply depressed. She intuits that her mother transforms her unhappiness into chronic physical symptoms without any physiological base. Marriage and children, as a life choice, does not look appealing to Miranda.

Miranda is afraid of becoming like her mother and unsure that she can hold the line against that happening. She is conflicted, because she loves her mother. "I know that if I don't get married and have children, she will be disappointed. But I tell myself that my sister has done exactly that and they've bonded over it. So I figure I need to make the right decision for me."

As she moves into her late twenties, she is doing the task of that decade, which is to develop her personal identity, including her morality, her sexual needs, her belief systems, and her work focus. For women like Miranda, the idea of marriage and children feels threatening to their hard-won identity. She does not want to give up who she is to become what society defines as a mother. A woman with complex issues has to make her way through them before she'll know for sure what her own best choice will be.

Miranda works for a women's rights organization, and her conservative parents are supportive. Still she says, "I'm the odd man out in my family. I'm the only one working in an office and the only one who thinks about larger issues." She admits that she looks up to her mother's sister and Larry's mom, who are both successful at work, more than she looks up to her own mother.

Recently, Miranda and Larry talked about having kids. Miranda has always said she didn't want them, but when she reiterated it this time, Larry said, with some surprise, "For real?" He'd always assumed it was "just something people did, and that we'd probably do it someday, too," Miranda says, with a laugh. "He wouldn't try to talk me into it. He doesn't really feel strongly about it, either."

Miranda and Larry have the same ethnic background and values. He has more Beta than she has, and she's had to nudge him to get his work life in order. "It's not my responsibility to tell him what to do," she says. "But he was jumping from job to job, and that was getting old. I'd tell him, 'Hey, your half of the rent is due, my friend!' I don't know if he would have gotten where he is today if it hadn't been for me, but ultimately, he did take advantage of something that fell into his lap. He has a good work ethic, and now he oversees a whole team of people."

In their relationship, she feels strongly that "you have to take care of yourself, but you don't have to take care of me. A lot of ideas people have about life are based on not doing what your parents did. I used to watch my father giving my mother an allowance, and that just killed me. It was so demeaning."

Gender deviation neutralization—when a woman breadwinner works harder than her partner at home—is still operative for Miranda and Larry, even though she consciously tries to avoid that trap. "When Larry wasn't working much and I'd come home and find the dishes in the sink, the disparity was too great. I'd get upset. Even as he's gotten busier, I'm still busier at home. He feels entitled not to do as much. I'll ask him, 'When was the last time you cleaned the bathroom?' He'll get defensive and say, 'What do you mean?' Then he does it. His feminist mom once apologized to me for not teaching him how to cook!"

Miranda finds it ironic that her best woman friend is following a traditional marriage path. "She's always saying how glad she is to know me because I'm different." How does this feel? Kind of good, kind of scary, too. Making choices that are considered different puts you out on a limb. As more of Miranda's peers get married, she sometimes wonders if it might not be so bad. "It would be a big concession for me, but if Larry felt it was really important, it's negotiable."

Miranda is more than capable of negotiating marriage on her own terms, as long as she feels sure that she isn't following in her mother's footsteps. Her self-confidence conceals a great deal of anxiety over issues of marriage and children. Coming from a dysfunctional traditional family, she's torn and tortured about her parents' relationship and especially about her mother. On the one hand she loves her mother, and on the other hand she has to reject her as a role model because she doesn't want to be like her—but this feels disloyal. Conflicted, Miranda makes a conscious charade of asking her mother's opinion on work issues—things she knows her mother knows nothing about.

Miranda needs to be aware that due to her mixed feelings about her mother she may end up with an unwanted pregnancy or a premature marriage: an unconscious way of easing, or resolving the extreme discomfort of the conflict. What this means is that instead of working it out, Miranda might *act* it out without realizing what she's doing. The only way for her to avoid this outcome is to be fully aware of her conflict, so that she makes clear, conscious choices—not confused, *un*conscious ones.

Miranda's choices are personal and political. As it is, she has a solid, loving relationship that gives her a secure base on which to make the best possible decisions for her.

LEVEL FIVE: ENGAGEMENT AND AFTER

We live in a culture of wedding overkill that leads people to believe that the perfect wedding will lead to the perfect life. All day, every day women are regaled by the Knot, *Brides* magazine, *Martha Stewart Weddings*, along with their websites and countless more wedding-devoted sites, as well as TV programs like *Say Yes to the Dress, My Fair Wedding*, and the entire Wedding Channel, where they are harangued by "celebrity" wedding gurus to buy, buy, buy. Probably, though, you will end up saying bye-bye to your savings.

No wonder some women turn into my-day-my-way divas. It can definitely bring out the worst Alpha qualities (revisit the questionnaire—control freak, anyone?). Consider whether your husband-to-be has suddenly become a prop; ensure that the two of you spend quality time together to check in about wedding-planning decisions, and even more important, your lives. Keep hold of the central importance of your relationship. Here's some healthy advice: spend time alone together every week, with a vow *not* to discuss wedding plans.

Take the wedding hype with several large grains of salt and instead consider some important and exciting new findings from the Council on Contemporary Families (CCF) about the egalitarian marriage.

In the 1950s, says Stephanie Coontz, the CCF's director of research and public education, a woman's best chance of a good marriage was to partner with a traditional, breadwinning male, while today, the traditional male (read: old-fashioned Alpha) is at greater risk of divorce than the men whom I've been talking about who value equal partnerships—the new Beta! This is very good news for everyone.

Keep that idea firmly in mind—and don't let your Alpha run amok into Bridezilladom. One groom-to-be had panic attacks when his fiancée shifted into high wedding gear. He felt overwhelmed as their relationship sank beneath things like engraved invitations, a seven-tier wedding cake, and a floral display that could fill Grand Central Station. Remember that the wedding business is just that—*business*. However, a *wedding* is, or should be, an event celebrating a couple's love and partnership with family and friends. Simple, really.

Because of the huge pressures of the engagement period, a couple's issues may come harshly to light. After my clients Peter and Eva became officially engaged, they nearly broke up. I was startled the day that Eva told me, in a conspiratorial tone while Peter was in the washroom, "I really want a *super*wedding." Why was she telling me this in her fiancé's absence? How was Peter going to be folded into her plans? Eva, an Alpha public relations executive who pushes her own agenda, is hard-charging at work and in her personal life. I knew her well enough to know that when she wanted something, she went after it—and usually got it.

As the other participant in your nuptials, your prospective husband comes first, but Eva wasn't paying the slightest attention to relationship dynamics. Instead she became increasingly swept up in wedding-planning culture. Riding a wave of excitement and self-indulgence, she began to organize a gala for three hundred guests, which included a formal sit-down dinner and a twelve-piece dance band. Peter, an architect, contributed by listening to band tapes and tagging along to look at venues. Eva didn't know it, but he was quietly keeping a running tab and becoming more and more agitated as she frittered money away on elaborate floral arrangements and Tiffany necklaces for her seven bridesmaids. As a strong Beta male, he was by far the more practical and cautious of the two; he believed they should be saving for a down payment on a house.

As an Alpha, Eva could be tone-deaf to other people's concerns when she chose to be. She felt especially self-confident and entitled because her career was on the rise. Why shouldn't she have her dream wedding? Meanwhile, Peter sensed correctly that the wedding was bringing into focus their differences about money and planning for the future. He dropped a few hints here and there, but Eva consciously ignored them and went on her merry way. Peter worried that their values were too far apart; still, he loved her and agonized over when and where to present his concerns, procrastinating until Eva was just about to put down a giant deposit on a huge loft space. Finally, he spoke up and let Eva know that her lavish spending was over-the-top and, furthermore, he wouldn't go along with it.

Fireworks ensued. Eva was astonished by his diligent tallying of what was supposed to be an "open budget," which Peter pointed out was an oxymoron. She accused him of being stingy and boring, and even threatened to break off the engagement. Had they come this far only to discover their values were an ocean apart? Maybe. They knew their relationship was on the brink, and that if they couldn't resolve this issue it was doomed.

Each retreated to his/her default position. Eva bullied, then cried. Peter tried to be rational. They started talking again, then backed off. They knew they loved each other, but the fault line in their relationship—Eva's tendency to dominate and Peter's complying to please her—was widening.

It wasn't easy, but over the next few weeks, having put everything, including the signing of the venue contract on hold, they tried to sort things out, averting disaster by airing their viewpoints, mirroring them back to each other, and, eventually, scaling down wedding costs and agreeing to save 10 percent of their combined income for a house.

Ultimately, the couple felt that their agreement reinforced their partnership. They spent more on the wedding than Peter liked, and Eva spent less than she wanted. But the real accomplishment was that they refocused on the reason they were getting married: they loved each other and wanted to make each other happy. Their short but intense power struggle served to remind them of what was important.

WHAT REALLY *IS* IMPORTANT

Whether you're living together with plans to marry, living together and engaged, or living separately and discussing marriage, the points on this checklist should give you an idea of how close you are as a couple to a real commitment.

- You are having good to great sex.

- You have met each other's families.

- You know each other's friends.

- You have separate lives but spend a large portion of your free time together.

- You talk to each other about personal and professional problems.

- You have had several disagreements about things that bother
  you, big and small, and your expectations of each other. And
  while this may not have been easy, you respected one another's
  point of view. Says Felicity, "Rick is a surfer, and when he was
  single, he got up at five AM to get out there. Finally, I said,
  'I don't care if the surf's up. I don't want you to go now. It's
  important to me that we spend time in bed.' He understood
  that. But I had to tell him, 'I *really* need you to do this.' People
  need to alter their routines. You aren't two single people living
  together; you're partnered. It's a bad sign if people can't do
  things that are important to the other person."

- You have a realistic sense of each other's faults, but you don't
  expect each other to be perfect. "There's no ideal guy," says a
  twenty-nine-year-old who lives with her boyfriend. "I found
  a man who's considerate and loving and makes me feel like a
  complete person. I don't need him to be a rock star."

- You have had serious conversations about the future, and
  you are both on the same page—you've hit all the big topics:
  money, sex, lifestyle, family, friends, children, and religion.
  Since differences on any of these can lead to marital discontent
  and tension, you're better off taking them on now, so that you
  can discover where there is overlap and consensus and where
  there is potential for conflict. If the discussions get heated,
  bravo! I applaud the brave ones who head out into open water
  and start to explore the unknown. Whatever you do, don't
  back away from these topics: even if you fear turning up deal
  breakers, you're likely to find that you can negotiate your
  different perspectives.

- You discuss marriage. If he is of a more traditional mind about it, he will want to propose—but it won't be a surprise. In fact, it will be more a question of *when* than *if.*

HOT BUTTON ISSUES

If you have hot-button issues, now is the time to take them on—and here is where your Alpha can really shine. You've never met a hot-button issue that seriously scares you. Dealing with sticky subjects requires honest, direct discussion—and your attitude is probably, Why shirk? Bring it on. Even more, if you combine your gutsiness with active listening (a positive Beta skill), you're in really good shape. Don't panic, even if you unearth some stubborn issues that you cannot resolve yourselves. You can consult a marriage therapist for help in understanding where you are stuck. Short-term premarital therapy is an excellent investment. So, get your Alpha together and confront it now rather than later.

As an example of tough topics, religion is one that swamps a lot of interfaith couples. With the rising numbers of mixed-faith marriages (now at 42 percent, according to a 2010 survey by Naomi Schaefer Riley), I see couples get blindsided by problems they hadn't expected. Two of my strong-willed Alpha clients, Zoe, thirty-four, and Luke, thirty-one, came to my office with their dilemma. The couple, who were engaged, had a great deal in common—from strong family ties to similar views on money to sexual compatibility—with one notable exception: religion. Zoe came from a fairly observant Jewish family, while Luke was raised as a Catholic. She always assumed her children would be raised as Jews and attend religious school with her siblings' children, and that Luke would convert.

Luke took the first step toward a discussion about their religious identities. Having started talking before coming to see me, they were well aware that this was going to be tough. Zoe was far more involved in her religion than Luke was in his, and she was much more certain about her vision of family life. Luke had a strong sense of self and knew how to take a stand; even though he was not religious, he felt that Catholicism was a part of him.

"I will agree to our children being Jewish," Luke said. "But I can't agree to religious school." Zoe hesitated—it was painful—but agreed to let that go as long as the kids were raised Jewish. Luke said that he would learn more about Judaism and participate in the Jewish holidays. He said that he would want them all to attend Mass at Christmas and to have a Christmas tree. Zoe cringed, saying she felt uncomfortable going to church and that the children would be confused. Still she agreed to celebrate Christmas and Easter with Luke's family.

During one session he quietly spoke about his feeling that she was denying the importance of his religious background. He was willing to participate in her beliefs (without converting), but he wanted his children to share in what mattered to him.

The couple's ability to listen respectfully and to understand the other's point of view strengthened the relationship. Zoe understood that by marrying outside of her religion, she had to be willing to compromise, and Luke had to reckon with his choice to marry a woman who highly valued a religious identity different from his own. Zoe was a strong advocate for herself, but Luke had an admirable ability to negotiate with sensitivity and clarity. Together, the couple took a leap of faith and avoided a deadly power struggle. After several weeks of discussion they eventually found common ground and both felt—as in all good deals—that they got some of what they wanted. They struck a good balance, and there was no ambiguity about the terms. Bravo for them!

BALANCE AND BOUNDARIES

Imagine a large, intricate mobile, with dangling pieces strung together at multiple levels, all ingeniously connected to create a delicate balance. Some pieces are closer to one another, others more peripheral. Even if the mobile sways, once the motion stops, the pieces realign and restabilize into the same configuration. Now picture the pieces of this mobile as members of your family of origin and of your important friendships. In relationship to each other, the pieces represent the dynamic interaction of family members and friends who make up your emotional connections.

When you commit to a serious relationship, you are adding a new piece (your partner) to the mobile, which throws it off-balance. You haven't just added a partner to *your* life, but to your entire family-and-friendship configuration! Now the mobile needs to be reconfigured to gain a new equilibrium, which means that the pieces have to be shifted around. New patterns are created, which you might not even be aware of. One thing is for sure: sticking to the old configuration will *not* accommodate the new piece. A family that is healthy and adaptable will maneuver their positions to get their so-called mobile back into balance.

You and your partner need to reconfigure all the relationships in your lives in both small and major ways. You may be very close to your parents and siblings, but as you make your partner a priority, you may have to modify your other relationships to make room. Conflicts of loyalty, when you're torn between your partner and someone else important to you, will seriously upset the mobile's balance.

At every stage in the life cycle—living together, marriage, parenthood, midlife changes, illness, a job loss, a job promotion, retirement—the mobile must be reorganized. So prepare to be adaptable and self-observant! There are plenty of challenges ahead, but it is exciting to think that you will be connected in new ways to the people you love. Who wants stasis anyway?

Alphas and Betas deal differently with their relationship mobiles. Betas, more attuned to relationships, may be more sensitive to other people's feelings and are likelier to accommodate additions (or subtractions). They perceive that people's feelings can be hurt, and they don't like seeing that happen. At the same time they may experience tension but not know quite how to handle it and may uneasily tolerate a state of imbalance. Alphas on the other hand may be high-handed and impatient with the realignments.

Sara was a case in point. She and her boyfriend Owen had met in college and spent their twenties living separately in different parts of the country as they built their careers, he as a lawyer, she as a doctor. She took a surgical residency in Los Angeles; he did a clerkship in Washington, DC. They considered themselves a couple and stayed monogamous, keeping their personal and professional goals front and center over the long-distance courtship. Recently, after they were established in their careers, they met up in New York and moved in together. They had been discussing engagement and marriage.

But Sara had a big problem with Owen's parents, and she knew they had to tackle it *before* they went any further. (For married people, in-law problems are insidious and one of the main causes of unhappiness and divorce.) Sara, an Alpha who reacts quickly and impatiently, said that Owen's parents were slighting her—and worse, Owen did not support her. She had decided that her future in-laws were *outlaws*. Owen looked forlorn as we discussed how Sara and his parents fought over him. He viewed himself as an innocent bystander in the war of the roses. As Sara listened and fumed, he explained that he was the baby of the family, and his mother doted on him. "What's so bad about that?" he defended himself. The couple defined the problem differently: Sara thought the issue was the parents, while Owen thought Sara should power down her anger and learn to understand them. This was a nonstarter.

The couple had known for a while that they had to resolve the tension between Sara and Owen's parents. But *resolve* is a multifaceted word, and each had different ideas about what it meant. Owen thought that Sara should back down and show his parents the respect they deserved. Sara took the bull-in-the-china-shop approach by insisting that Owen give his parents the cold shoulder until they came around. Obviously the two resolves were unresolvable.

"They are so difficult," she complained. "Last week I exploded at them because I wanted to plan Owen's thirtieth birthday party, and they told me they were already doing it! They implied that they knew what he wanted and I didn't. How dare they treat me this way? I have had enough!" In our first interview I knew I'd spotted a super-Alpha female on the march. She wanted a showdown between herself and Owen and his parents. "I think we need to confront the issue head-on," she said. "They think I am taking their son away."

Owen adored his parents, but he had found his own quiet ways to keep them at a distance. Although they called him several times every day, he "never told them anything," so in his mind he was independent. Previously he'd never confronted their tendency to baby him. He hated the direct approach, and it seemed to him that being passive was fine, as long as it didn't keep him from doing what he wanted—as it hadn't until now.

It had never occurred to Owen that he was part of the problem, and I thought that he had to put himself in the equation. He was loving and available to Sara, but he had to face his passivity—a common negative Beta trait—in a situation that demanded action. I challenged his innocence and asked him to step back from his own behavior so he could observe how he perpetuated the ambiguity of his relationship with Sara. I asked Owen: How did he want his parents to treat Sara?

How had he defined his and Sara's relationship to his parents? Had he made it clear to his parents how important Sara was to him? When Sara fought with his parents did he feel he had to choose between them? He finally had to admit that his separation from his family was incomplete.

Still, nothing happened, and Sara's frustration erupted again. "I want you to cut off contact with them!" she demanded.

"With his mother and father?" I asked, disbelieving. "Sara, you are asking Owen to choose between you and his parents. That's an untenable choice."

Then I turned to Owen. "You need to let your parents know that Sara is a serious partner, possibly a future wife, and that you want them to treat her respectfully. After all, you picked a feisty, intense woman, so that's something that you love and need. Borrow some of it and talk to your parents."

As Owen stepped up to the plate, Sara threw her bat away, at first, reluctantly. Then, in a shift toward generosity and humility, she told his parents that she had contributed to the tension and that she wanted to get along with them. They were so stunned that they agreed to work together to resolve their issues.

"I can deal with them," Sara said, "if they are respectful and know their place."

A few weeks ago, after the couple left therapy, I received an announcement of their engagement. Sara attached a PS: "Owen's mother and I will never be best friends, but we are all getting along much better."

Imagine that relationship mobile again. The parents had to add Sara and rebalance; Sara had to add them to her configuration. At first things went wildly out of whack; it took guts and finesse to create something new.

These problems almost always involve boundaries: how to draw a circle around your relationship so that you are exclusive to one another, while also maintaining a relationship with your families of origin. Not so easy.

THE PRESSURE IS ON

"You can do better." This was the whispered message in my client's ear at a party, after she had introduced her boyfriend to a married woman friend. At the friend's self-confident pronouncement, she stopped in her tracks, outraged by this snap judgment and sneakily anxious that her friend might be right. She was shaken. The rest of the evening was shot.

"How do you know he'll be successful?" "You'll always make more money than he does." "Don't you think you might be, kind of, marrying down?" Many Alpha women who choose Beta men are faced with these kinds of remarks, suggestions, observations, or whatever you want to call them, from friends, families, and colleagues. You may be sensitive to the things people say and to the implications that a man is somehow beneath you and that you've sold yourself short. After all, you've been taught to value ambition and accomplishment, and you've probably also been raised to believe that a wealthy, hard-charging Alpha male will be your most suitable husband.

What if a man you like isn't the most ambitious guy in his field? What if he hasn't set his sights on climbing the corporate ladder? What if he has other values? It's a cliché, but let's say it anyway. Money isn't everything, nor is success in the corporate world. There are women executives married to elementary school teachers, women physicians married to stay-at-home dads, women clergy married to musicians, women entrepreneurs married to nurses or physical therapists, and so on.

If other people's remarks get under your skin and cause tension in your relationship, consider this: you may be vulnerable to criticism because you have a critical parent—and that's whose voice you hear beneath all the other voices. So do a quick self-examination:

- Does your boyfriend have a good work ethic and some serious ambition to do well in his chosen field?
- Does he respect you and share your values and vision of life?
- Do you respect his work?
- Do the two of you have fun together?
- Are you intellectual equals? Do you share interests?
- Do you have good sex?
- Would you rather be with him than anyone else?

If your answer to these questions is yes, then who is anyone else to judge your choice? Other people don't know what's right for you. When one woman was repeatedly asked how she knew her fiancé, who was not on a corporate trajectory, would be successful, she replied, "Well, I don't know that for sure, but I think he's great. If we need more money, I will make it."

Draw that invisible boundary line around your relationship. Then shut down the voices of dissent and believe in yourself, in him, and in the two of you together.

POWER SHARING WITH THE BETA MAN

In a healthy relationship, power must be fairly allotted. Both partners get equal time to talk and to listen. Partnership trumps power! Alphas, beware.

Alphas are used to leading and making decisions—and this is usually a positive attribute. But in relationships, they can be overpowering. Alphas may dig their heels in until their partner is worn out. They may belittle or mock their partner's arguments. They want to win. I've seen all of these patterns of behavior in my office, and trust me, they will seriously interfere with your ability to resolve your differences.

Therapists talk about a dynamic called negative complementarity, in which each person becomes an extreme, calcified version of him- or herself. Instead of helping each other improve, they covertly or openly blame the other for his/her shortcomings. So an Alpha becomes domineering and controlling (as opposed to leading), and a Beta becomes sulky and resentful instead of collaborative. (Two Betas might need to challenge each other more, while two Alphas might need to be less combative and more compromising.)

In positive complementarity, partners learn to borrow some of each other's positive qualities. An Alpha woman can balance out her edginess and tendency to dominate by borrowing some of her Beta guy's ability to compromise. Meanwhile, he can borrow from her a more direct approach to problem solving. Both partners can provide the space for negative qualities to be softened or areas of weakness strengthened.

Power sharing involves mutual honesty, respect, and clarity. Before you discuss something that bothers you or make an important decision, you both need to:

1. Create a caring atmosphere where it is safe to raise concerns.
2. Be receptive to what the other has to say.
3. Be committed to seeing your partner's point of view.
4. Monitor your tone and content to maximize trust and goodwill.
5. Avoid sarcasm and snide remarks.
6. Avoid lecturing.
7. Put past resentments aside and work from a positive point of view.
8. Recognize that compromise is the best solution to problems.
9. Allow yourself to feel vulnerable when you talk about your feelings.
10. Commit to finding acceptable solutions and understand that winning an argument can actually mean losing the relationship.

CHAPTER 7

AFFAIRS: PERFECT STORMS

IF CHEATING WAS ONCE primarily the prerogative of Alpha males, it certainly has gone much further than that now. The moral code against adultery has been weakened by the culture of instant gratification. Why not do it if everyone else is? Since the 1970s, women's cheating has steadily risen, and now women reportedly stray almost as much as men do, according to new research. All kinds of explanations for this phenomenon are being floated. Kristen Mark, the lead author of a 2011 Indiana University study, said that for women, not being happy in a relationship and not being sexually compatible made them more likely to stray.

There are more reasons. When a woman has an independent career, professional achievements, and a good income, she is not afraid of divorce. She has more control over her life than a woman who is financially dependent. But this doesn't necessarily mean that a woman's infidelity is particularly likely to cause divorce; in fact, a career woman who has affairs is not usually looking to divorce her partner.

She is simply behaving as men have in the past—taking advantage of an empowered position. The Alpha woman is more adventure seeking and feels more entitled to her own happiness, so if she is sexually bored, she feels that it is her right to seek some excitement. Even if her marriage *did* end over her affairs, she'd know she'd be fine, financially.

Women are out in the workplace, where sexual tensions can quickly intensify with regular contact. And when opportunity does not readily present itself, there are special websites catering to extramarital sexual relationships. The sites feature photos from the neck down—no head shots to expose anyone's identity. I was surprised to find that one site claims to have 17 million members in twenty-five countries. Interesting!

It may also be true that when all is said and done, women's sexuality is not so different from men's. A 2010 study by Hyde and Petersen at the University of Wisconsin found that when men and women are more equal within the culture, "most gender differences in sexual attitudes and behaviors [are] small." Contrary to the claim that men are more promiscuous and the assumption that they are therefore more likely to cheat, the most recent studies argue that women are not innately monogamous either. Some recent research at the Center for Sexual Medicine at Sheppard Pratt shows that more women than men suffer from what is called hypoactive sexual-desire disorder (HSDD), a lack of libido within a relationship. Today's married women may view monogamous sex as a bit humdrum after the excitement of their sex lives before marriage.

But if it's easy to carry on an affair in the digital age, it's even *easier* to get caught. Who hasn't snooped on their partner? In a survey of two thousand people conducted by a dating website, 36 percent of young adults thought it was OK. There is a serious moral issue with secretly reading someone's private e-mails or texts, and it doesn't make it all right because a lot of people do it. But with technology, privacy has gone out of fashion; it's literally outdated. Everything you post on the web, whether it's a blog or a picture of your dog on Facebook, or, God forbid, a photo of your private parts, is out there. And some of it will haunt us for a long time.

Another reason we snoop is simply because we can. We actually feel entitled to invade our partner's privacy. In a perverse way, we have grown to expect the worst from our partners, because we too have been tempted to secretly flirt or hide something in an e-mail or a text. We snoop to find out what our partner is up to because we know how easy it is to be indulgent in a culture that provides instant gratification and overstimulation. Loyalty to a partner clashes with the impulsive nature of the digital world.

I think of affairs as marital perfect storms. Picture a relationship hit by a combination of circumstances that together create a huge event with intense repercussions. At one time or another, almost every marriage is vulnerable to an affair. Whether you call it sexual ennui, disinterest, or dissatisfaction, the root cause lies within the relationship. And it takes two: the internal circumstances for an affair are always created by the *couple*. Opportunities external to the relationship add unprecedented power to personal turmoil.

Still, according to a *Wall Street Journal* article, up to 80 percent of marriages survive an affair. Whether a marriage endures almost always depends upon both partners developing an understanding of the causes and what personal (i.e., midlife) and interpersonal (marital) issues contributed. The couple must work together at rebuilding and making their marriage stronger. One person can't do it alone.

ALPHA AFFAIRS, BETA AFFAIRS

Different personality types have different kinds of affairs. Let's say that a Beta woman and her Alpha husband have an exciting courtship and a happy early marriage, but after the birth of their second child, the couple grows apart. She is somewhat disappointed in her marriage and secretly angry with him, because she feels he's not interested in what she is doing and does not try to understand her. She occasionally fantasizes about a relationship with someone who is receptive and affectionate. At the same time she misses the old chemistry with her husband and wishes she could pop a pill and feel lust the way she used to.

As the head of fund-raising at the PTA, she meets another active parent, a father, and they start going out for coffee. They find that they share a similar sense of humor and enjoy regaling each other with stories about the quirky parents at school or the latest funny YouTube video making the rounds. Before too long, they confide that their marriages are lackluster, which intensifies their intimacy. Unconscious of the fact that her unexpressed anger toward her husband is fueling her emotions, she becomes increasingly involved with her friend. What she doesn't *consciously* realize is that having an affair would be a good way of getting back at her husband.

When she fantasizes about having sex with her friend, she admonishes herself: "What am I thinking? I would never do that." But never is a long time, and soon they acknowledge their feelings toward each other. The smoldering sexual tension gets the better of them, they begin an affair, and her self-confidence gets a great boost. She rediscovers a sense of herself as sexy and desirable, not to mention better equipped to stand up to her husband.

While an Alpha can shrug off misgivings, a Beta has an appropriate sense of guilt, and before too long things get messy. She doesn't have the temperament for an easy fling, and meanwhile her common sense tells her that she will eventually be found out. It is high-anxiety time. The affair comes to a painful end.

Sometimes guilt kicks in when you don't expect it to. Liz, a married friend of mine, ran into a man she'd worked with years ago in a newsroom. They had lunch and traded war stories about the past. As they chatted about their families, she recalled with some nostalgia their close, sometimes flirtatious—but always platonic—friendship. As they parted, he casually mentioned a blog that he'd started some time ago. At home, she searched for the blog and saw that he'd been posting his sexual fantasies about her, including detailed descriptions of her body.

For a shy Beta woman, this exposure was awful. She felt stalked and betrayed and very angry; strangely, she also felt guilty, as if she'd done something wrong—as if in fact she'd actually had an affair. Her instinct was to cut off all contact by blocking further e-mails or texts, but feeling unsure, she asked me what I thought. I was certain her instinct was right. Engaging him in an e-mail back-and-forth really wasn't her style. Her silent message was clear: don't contact me. In the tech world, strange stuff can happen, but no, you're not guilty by unwittingly playing a role in someone else's online fantasy life.

KILLER INSTINCT

The business world offers up cheating opportunities that may be nearly impossible to resist. Alphas are more susceptible to temptation for the simple reason that they are, by temperament, drawn to challenge, adventure, and stimulation like bees to honey. For decades business-men have conducted out-of-town dalliances; now Alpha women are susceptible as well. The boisterous atmosphere of business conferences creates a perfect storm for the Alpha who is impulsive, risk-prone, and unabashed about her appetite for sex. Fueled and disinhibited by booze, she may find herself flirting with a sexy guy. The two of them are, in equal parts, seducer and seduced. She doesn't want to stop because it feels so good, and soon they've ended up in a hotel room.

Afterward, she may feel a guilty twinge or two, but she'll rationalize the fling as harmless. She vows never to do it again, because she knows it is wrong, but quickly forgets the incident. An Alpha-style fling rarely gets messy.

My client, Caitlin, a fashion magazine publisher, is a tiny, dark-haired powerhouse of a woman, with a wide-eyed look and a charming manner. She dresses with great style, including stilettos with hidden platforms that add several inches to her height. Caitlin was brought up in a family that scrambled to pay the bills, and she learned the hard way how to survive and thrive. She did well enough in school to win scholarships to college. She arrived at adulthood priding herself on being tough and getting ahead. With her degree, corporate America beckoned.

She met Michael, an attractive fashion photographer, in the lobby of a Midtown office building. He loved her energy and ambition, and she admired his creativity and his romantic, somewhat tortured artistic sensibility. The sex was crackling, and as time went on, they discovered somewhat to their surprise that they shared some traditional beliefs and values about family life. Marriage wasn't far off.

By the time Caitlin and Michael came to see me for a marital tune-up, as they put it, they had two children. Caitlin was putting in long, hard hours at her job, and she'd been regularly promoted. She not only loved the work but also the competitive, high-risk environment. She considered herself "one of the guys" at the office and on the road. Meanwhile, Michael had been forced to give up his studio during the recession when advertising work dried up and now stayed home with the kids, carving out a niche for himself as the founder of a neighborhood parenting group. He'd discovered, he said, that he actually liked his life as it was, and in fact the couple had achieved a deal that worked for them: Caitlin, the Alpha breadwinner, Michael, the stay-at-home Beta dad. They barely saw each other from one weekend to the next, but their sexual relationship was still hot. They kept in touch throughout the day by text, even if it was just to say, "I love you."

Then Michael discovered some personal, sexy messages from a colleague on Caitlin's phone, which opened a Pandora's box of troubles. Caught red-handed, Caitlin confessed that she'd had a fling, hastening to assure Michael that it "hadn't meant anything." But she was in trouble at work, too. Recently, she'd been reamed out by her top boss for overextending the limits of her expense account. On business trips she'd been staying in the most expensive hotels and entertaining lavishly. Defensively, she told us she was under a lot of pressure and felt entitled to spend money. At a recent retirement party for a woman colleague, Caitlin learned that over the course of her career the woman had brought in a billion dollars of revenue; this had whetted her competitive appetite, and she'd vowed to do even better. By now, tales of her business expenses and her personal life provided endless grist for the office gossip mill.

Things got even wilder. Her company censured her for inappropriate behavior, then suspended her. (Can you imagine any of this happening if she'd *really* been one of the guys? I don't think so!) Not that Caitlin folded—to the contrary. The censure brought out her killer instinct, and she hired one of the toughest employment lawyers in town, who threatened a sexual discrimination suit if she were fired. She won the case and left, under her own steam, for a more senior position at another company.

Now Michael had post-affair angst. Cuckolded Alpha males usually seek divorce as a way to deflect humiliation and rejection, but as a Beta, Michael's behavior was different. Generally content with his role in the marriage, in awe of his wife, and dependent on her breadwinning role, he felt compelled to find a way to be forgiving. Threatened, he acted to solidify his position, and instead of challenging her and overtly showing his unhappiness, he immediately redoubled his efforts to be an adoring mate—as many women will do to win back a wandering husband.

Caitlin was bothered enough to come for individual therapy. She knew she'd gone too far, both personally and professionally, and that she needed to reset her moral compass. There are certain steps to take to strengthen a marriage like this one. When one or both partners work long hours, they need to check in with each other, with more than a quick text, on a regular basis—especially, but not only, when one of them is out of town. Think of it as a way to download the day, deal with problems, and, overall, stay close. It's a reminder that in spite of the demands, opportunities, and temptations of the outside world, the relationship is primary. For highfliers like Caitlin, affairs will always be a temptation, but she needs to respect and value the man managing the home fort.

The couple, who are at the opposite ends of the Alpha/Beta continuum, have to create a balance between her recklessness and his caution. This is the particular vulnerability of their partnership, and the more they are aware of that, the better they can protect it. Creating marital and family rituals will keep them close, despite challenging circumstances. The tether of respect and loyalty will be what binds them over the long term.

PRIDE OF THE BAD BOY

Before he married Nancy, Nick lived large and had things his way. Disdaining a regular job after graduating from college, he headed out West, to Sin City, where he became a poker-playing high roller. Nick took to Las Vegas like a duck to water and would have stayed there happily laying bets forever, had he not been recruited aggressively by several Wall Street firms. He packed up and went back East, ending up a few years later in a top position in a big firm. Time after time he got into trouble for ultrarisky decisions, until he was finally banished from work for two years. For that bad-boy behavior, Nick was hailed as a hero on the Street.

Along the way he'd fallen in love with and married Nancy, a smart, solid Beta, who provided an earthbound counterweight to his extreme Alpha tendency to fly too close to the sun. She worried about his hubris—overbearing pride—and told him not to brag about his scrapes with the law. She felt he should not wear his punishment as a badge of honor.

Things got worse after Nancy discovered his affairs. A month before Christmas, she had found prettily tied boxes from Chanel and Tiffany tucked into the back of the closet. She'd assumed they were for her, but Christmas came and went and, oddly, the boxes never made an appearance. One day soon after that, on his way to take a shower, Nick tossed his cell phone on the bed. Nancy happened to walk into the bedroom just as a text popped up. She picked up the phone and found texts from two or three women. After getting his phone records from Verizon, she cross-referenced the calls with the texts and wasted no time in confronting him.

In therapy we discussed how Nick's fiftieth birthday was around the corner, and that he was fighting intimations of mortality: for the first time in his life, Nick felt vulnerable. Because he looked younger than his age, it wasn't hard for him to attract younger women—and temporarily soften the blow of a receding hairline and a bad left knee. Nancy made it clear in an early session that she was ready to walk if he didn't own up and show remorse for his dalliances. She was clear about what she would tolerate and what she would not, and what that came down to was no second chances. Nick, who loved her very much and understood on some level that she stabilized him emotionally, knew he had to toe the line. Even so, getting over the crisis was just the beginning of the recovery process: they spent a year in therapy rebuilding their relationship.

Because Nancy knew that the relationship was at risk, she made a smart decision by not being wishy-washy about what she would and would not tolerate. By doing so, she strengthened their bond. Nick was faced with a stark choice: the relationship or more uncertainty than he was prepared to live with. Instead of crashing and burning, the humbled highflier was floating gradually down to earth.

"IT'S ONLY A TEXT"

At thirty-five, Allison was looking for a relationship, and she met Dave online. She was open about her goal being a serious relationship and then marriage, and Dave, in his early forties, agreed that he was looking for something serious as well. He was taken with Allison because she was very attractive—not the kind of woman who was usually interested in him. More Omega than Beta, Dave was cute and boyish but wishy-washy. As a teenager and in college he'd been unpopular with girls, but had discovered that with his law degree he was a babe magnet: plenty of women were interested in hooking up with him. (That was probably why he became a lawyer in the first place; he wasn't especially hardworking or interested in the work.) With his lawyer chops, Dave started taking full advantage of the hookup culture. Two years into the relationship Allison and Dave had a crisis.

When Allison saw Dave's phone on the kitchen counter signaling a message, she picked it up. "I don't know why," she said. "Something made me do it." Sure enough, she discovered a bunch of sexy messages. Far more Beta than Alpha, Allison had to push herself to confront Dave. With my support in a couple's session, she finally said, "I can't believe you'd do this! I feel totally betrayed."

"Wait," Dave argued. "I haven't seen anyone else since I've been with you. Look, it's *only* a text!"

I tried to get Dave to understand that "it's only a text" just didn't cut it. He had violated Allison's trust—but he didn't see it that way. Not grasping that his behavior was deceitful, he returned again and again to his rationale. As I struggled to understand his perspective, I realized that the ambiguity of texting allows you to participate in behavior that simultaneously distances you from that very behavior. In this way, Dave's actions belonged to a disembodied form of Dave, not the real Dave. And if this meta-Dave weren't real, then the real Dave didn't have to take responsibility. Beware! This kind of reasoning can wreck a relationship: who is this person—really?

In our sessions together, we worked toward more transparency between Allison and Dave. Eventually, though, Allison chose to end it. Trust is the foundation of a relationship, and she knew it wasn't there and probably never would be. It was a risky bet. Way too risky. As I said earlier in the book, *don't settle*. Read the handwriting on the wall, cut your losses, and leave. "Go girl!" I thought.

And within a year, Allison was in love with someone else—who shared her goals.

SEXUAL BURNOUT

Divorce survivors, Juli, thirty-four, and Bradley, thirty-seven, met online. Bradley was a Manhattan opthalmologist who lived in an apartment overlooking Central Park, while Juli led a casual, somewhat bohemian lifestyle in a diverse neighborhood in Queens.

For the first several months, they explored each other's neighborhoods and went to films, museums, and restaurants. Bradley, a self-confident, determined Alpha with a brusque manner, took the lead in deciding on destinations and dinners. They put off sexual involvement just to be sure they both wanted to be in a new relationship. Finally, one night after a fabulous dinner and two bottles of expensive wine, they had sex.

Juli, a Beta who always entered relationships with raw emotion and a knack for attaching quickly, was swept off her feet, and soon the couple decided that they would live together. They were both surprised at how strong the sexual attraction was and how much they enjoyed each other's company. With something like amazement, they realized they were madly in love. Outside the relationship things were going smoothly as well. Juli was part of a group crafts show in Brooklyn, and Bradley's practice was gaining in clients and popularity.

Then came trouble. After a year of living together, their sexual desire burned out, or at least Bradley's did. They were clearly an affectionate couple, so what had gone wrong? A sexless relationship is very vulnerable, whether it is one person who is disinterested or both. Then they told me that they wanted to have a baby. I was pleased for them but wary; clearly, something was wrong. Shouldn't they resolve the relationship first? But before I could say slow down, Juli was pregnant. The couple left therapy, and some months later, I received a beautiful engraved birth announcement and, after that, regular updates on the baby's milestones.

When I next saw Juli and Bradley, three years had passed, and they were in a crisis. They'd decided to have an open marriage, and both were involved sexually with other people. An affair can strike right into the vulnerable heart of a relationship, and in this case that is exactly what happened. Juli freaked out when she understood that Bradley had fallen in love with the woman he was seeing. In session, he told Juli that even though he loved her, he simply could not reset the sex button. His voice was firm, but I could see the pain it caused him to say this.

"But I'm in love with you," Juli protested. "I'll do whatever I have to do to make things better. Please, let's work on our relationship." I saw how desperate she was to make Bradley love her. Juli was so much the needier and less self-confident of the pair that the power balance was dangerously off-kilter.

Bradley could only repeat what he'd said, in as honest and loving way as possible: "I love you, Juli, but I'm not sexually attracted to you. I can't 'work' on sex if the attraction isn't there." It was brutal—even though he hadn't intended it that way.

Even when partners agree to sleep with other people, there is always an undertow of jealousy, resentment, and hurt feelings, and in this case, Juli, who was pursuing and being repeatedly rejected, was drowning. It *was* brutal. The couple has now separated, which is extremely painful for both. The real core of the problem was their long-standing sexual ennui, which they tried to treat with an open relationship. This bit of bait and switch gave them the psychological room to avoid confronting their sexual problem. Letting other people into their dyad had smoked out its hidden dysfunctional piece.

CAN YOU KEEP A SECRET? *SHOULD* YOU?

In some cases, as with Tricia and Sanders, serious relationship unhappiness and sexual boredom leads to an affair, which may then provide an opportunity to reinvest in a marriage. But a perfect storm like this one may not end as calmly as you'd like it to.

Married for seven years, the couple's sexual relationship was great in the beginning but proceeded to burn itself out in their ongoing explosive conflicts. Tricia had a brief affair at one point, which she'd confessed to Sanders and for which he'd forgiven her, though with great difficulty: he was a straight arrow with high moral principles. After that, sparks continued to fly; unfortunately, as the years passed, those sparks often blazed into open hostility.

Tricia's long blond hair frames her heart-shaped face; at thirty-eight this edgy Alpha is a knockout. Sanders, equally attractive, is a political analyst who works on big campaigns and has a reputation for devising brilliant strategies. Tricia and Sanders are the parents of a boy and a girl in elementary school. From all appearances, the pair seems to be the perfect couple. But when they stepped into my office, they were frazzled, frustrated, and furious with each other.

It was a classic case of two Alphas locking horns. Everything was a battle, from whether to open an expensive bottle of wine for dinner (she wanted to; he didn't) to which route to take home from a "relaxing" drive in the country (he wanted scenic; she wanted the thruway), to anything and everything else. Their arguments, fueled by high-octane personality power, frightened their children, so after about four sessions, we came to a decision that the couple would take a break and cool off.

Sometimes a couple just needs some space to get a stress-free perspective and regain an inner balance. I usually suggest spending three to six months apart, to see if we can neutralize the battle zone and achieve a détente. But I always insist on a *structured* separation in which I try to negotiate the terms in as much detail as possible. For instance: Would they have an option to date other people? Or would they keep the relationship monogamous? How would they manage childcare and caretaking?

This turned out to be the easy part. They agreed to put the children's needs first. To avoid disturbing their kids' living arrangement, they rented a studio apartment at the end of the block, and took turns living there. They also agreed to allow themselves the option to socialize, but not to have sex with anyone else. All this was accomplished smoothly with a lot of goodwill. So far, so good, I thought.

Indeed, the separation brought relief from fighting and much-needed peace to the relationship. The couple traded off seeing their children in a cooperative and thoughtful manner. As they started socializing separately but not romantically, they found they liked their independence. They had the emotional space to concentrate on their careers and their children. As their lives settled into the new routine, they decided to give themselves more time on their own before they began to consider where the relationship would go. For that reason they took a break from therapy.

About six months later, they realized that they missed each other and decided to spend time together at home and with their children. They kept the studio for sleeping. As they grew more comfortable, they found they could communicate more directly with a lot less tension and rediscovered their strong connection. This told them that they were ready to segue back to living together and resuming their sexual relationship. At the one-year mark, the family was reunited.

They returned for some brief therapy. This time around we focused on how to identify their unconstructive default positions in the way they related to each other. Each identified his or her my-way-or-the-highway behavior. Tricia recognized that she needed to manage her razor-sharp hot temper while Sanders admitted that he had to allow his cool rationalism to melt down a little. It is hard work for a couple, particularly two Alphas, to own up to, and to work on, their fatal flaw as a couple: in this case the habitual perilous pattern of escalating tensions. Each made a promise to him- and herself to alter the pattern. Finally they felt they had made significant progress and agreed to stop therapy.

When clients feel ready to go it alone, I always encourage them while letting them know that should they run into difficulty they can return. (By the way, therapists should never suggest or insinuate that ending therapy is a bad idea. Even if the therapist feels it is ill-advised, she should give clients her blessing. A client should *always* be in charge of his or her own therapy.)

I felt that Tricia and Sanders were on a very good footing when they left, and that's why, several months later, I was surprised to hear from Tricia. The moment she walked in, she broke down in tears and told me that in the early days of the separation, she'd hooked up with an old friend of hers and Sanders's. It happened in a way that often happens for Alphas. She was at a party and, as people gradually began drifting out, she stayed, enjoying her newfound freedom. Soon, she was alone with the old friend, and very drunk and giddy. The sexual tension was at peak level, and finally they had hours of great, uninhibited sex.

In the ensuing months, as Tricia reconnected with her husband, she was haunted by her impulsive behavior, which had been her nemesis all her life. She was in agony as she realized that she had done something that could not be undone, and she knew, absolutely, that this time around Sanders would not forgive her.

We discussed the long- and short-term consequences for the marriage and, most crucially, whether she should tell her husband. Repeatedly, she insisted that if Sanders found out, their stability would fall apart and it would be her fault. She didn't want to tell him. Often, people will rationalize lying to a partner by saying that telling the truth would create more harm than good. Almost always, I encourage people to come clean with their partner, take the consequences, and ask for forgiveness. How can we justify lying when we all know that relationships are built on trust?

But in this case we had to carefully weigh the pros and cons of that generally sound strategy. I wanted to know just how likely it was that she'd be exposed. Had her lover ever bragged to anyone about the sexual encounter? Were people talking about her? When she said she didn't think these things were likely to happen, I made a deliberate decision not to urge her to come clean because I agreed that the relationship might not survive a disclosure. In the end, it was Tricia's call to make, and she decided to stay mum and endure the shame and guilt. In a way she was choosing to punish herself for her impulsive behavior—but the punishment of telling Sanders seemed even worse.

Relationships are complex, and sometimes *not* adhering to the generally accepted wisdom is the best or only way through a bad situation. Tricia's new sense of self-awareness and fallibility was hard-won but meaningful. For some dilemmas there are no easy resolutions, and Tricia's was one of those.

"THE ZONE OF OVERLAPPING CLOSENESS"

Sounds like something to do with a business deal, doesn't it? Well, actually, it's a term that applies to couples who are trying to make another kind of deal. They are attempting to find the zone where their differing needs for closeness and distance are satisfied. When the zone is out of whack, the relationship is vulnerable to a destructive episode.

Due to temperament and upbringing, each of us is wired in a particular way when it comes to how much closeness and distance we require. Some of us need a steady diet of affirmation, appreciation, and affection; others need independence and companionship with less emotional involvement. Intuitively, you might judge the former to be correct. After all, relationships are supposed to be intimate. Actually, though, neither one is right or wrong.

In the first year of a relationship, a couple should seek the right balance *for them*. I met Brian and Cynthia several years into their marriage, and I quickly saw that they had never completed that initial all-important task. In their early time together, they'd seen their relationship as a place for them to heal from nasty divorces. Everything was new and wonderful. Then the bloom was off the rose.

Hot-tempered and provocative, they baited each other with sarcastic remarks and name-calling, with the anger escalating dangerously.

And there they were: two high-functioning professionals scrapping like kids on a playground.

When a couple comes in at this level of anger the first thing I do is teach them the eight signs of "anger arousal": rapid breathing and heart rate, clenched fists, ignoring what the other is saying, talking over each other, escalating voice volume, getting into each other's space, gesturing and pointing fingers. By recognizing these signs you are now in a position to *de*-escalate the situation. I taught the couple to take a timeout: go into separate rooms for at least one hour; take a walk in the park to decompress; agree not to talk about the subject until after a cooling-off period. Dialogue *cannot* happen when you are in an aroused state.

Once Brian and Cynthia had mastered these behaviors, we dug out the underlying reasons for their mutual rage. Brian was the pursuer, seeking more contact, affection, and interaction. Meanwhile, Cynthia withdrew by working long hours and reading her law journals into the wee hours. (Once again, traditional female and male stereotypes don't apply!) Brian expressed his hurt feelings through anger, and Cynthia felt criticized and blamed, which initially made her withdraw further. Then, when she felt cornered, she struck back.

Things got better, but in truth, they never settled into the right relationship temperature. What was comfortable for her was too cold for him; what was warm enough for him was too hot for her. Over time, they adjusted their expectations to the lowest bar. Brian was the unhappier partner, but he loved Cynthia and did not want to divorce. Still, he was lonely and craved affection.

And he found it.

One day, as he was sitting in a bar having dinner by himself, a lovely, much younger woman who was in New York on business sat down next to him. They struck up a conversation, and you take it from there. He was like low-hanging fruit, ripe for the picking. Brian is likable and sophisticated, and he could tell she admired his business acumen. He was charmed by her intelligence, easygoing manner, and warmth; she was the anti-Cynthia. They began a carefree, casual relationship in which they saw each other several times a month, when she traveled to New York on business.

This is going to sound cynical, but bear with me. An affair can sometimes lend ballast to a vulnerable marriage. Suddenly, the tension is gone! The partner having the affair is visibly happier, while the other partner is probably a little relieved; on some level she knows what is going on, but now she has the freedom to stay at the office as late as she wants without feeling pressured. The partner having the affair is thankful not to be sexually rejected or given dutiful sex. The new status quo suits everybody, for a while. No one is the culprit: the three players in the drama are all in bed together.

Do I think Brian and Cynthia's arrangement will last? Not for long. Looking the other way is a delicate balance that can only be maintained by an unspoken agreement between the parties. It almost never solves the problem in the long term. The most likely outcome in this situation is that the affair will be exposed (most likely via a vibrating cell phone or the ping of a text), and the couple will divorce after ugly accusations and bitterness. In this scenario, the wife will probably avoid taking responsibility for her coldness by constructing the narrative that she is the victim of a cheating husband. The husband will blame his wife for driving him into an affair. Everyone will feel wronged.

The best way to avoid instability is to note the warning signs ahead. If one person feels neglected by a lack of interest or affection, or if the other person feels she does not have enough space, there is going to be trouble. The couple needs to find the sweet spot of mutual satisfaction. Neither gets exactly what he or she wants, but once they're in the zone, they get enough.

The sexual bond between partners should be primary and sacred. Affairs, driven by impulsivity, dissatisfaction, lust, and anger, may invade a marriage like a force of nature. But affairs don't just happen. There are causes to understand and choices to make. Together, you have more control than you may think.

CHAPTER 8

DIVORCING, DATING, SURVIVING, THRIVING

NOWADAYS THERE ARE MANY ways to get what you want without compromising your integrity, and women are thinking out of the box and taking risks. It's all about using your Alpha skills, not just to survive but also to thrive. For Alphas moving toward and through the decade of their thirties, life is becoming more complicated than ever. You are looking for the right partner, getting engaged, marrying, having children, working, and trying to establish a good work-family balance. Or you're divorcing, planning to remarry and create a blended family, or thinking about raising your children alone. You're getting back into the dating game or taking time out. You may be considering a plan B—adopting or using technology to help ensure fertility.

I will talk about some of the many, many women who don't have typical married lives with children. So many of my Alpha clients, who seem so secure on the surface, are extremely anxious: how to fit in everything they want, how to make the right choices, how to tap into the resilience they need to deal with unexpected events. In this chapter I will talk about recovery from life's losses and all the surprising, unconventional, and wholly legitimate forms your recovery may take.

○ ○ ○ ○

Damn the biological clock:

"When do I find the time to have a baby? One of my co-workers said at a meeting, 'Do you mind if I pump?' I don't care if she does it, but I don't want to do that at work!"

—*Miranda*

"Until now I never wanted to have kids. But I've been married two years, and I've changed. I want three kids; I have to get started." —*Yvette*

"I'm busy trying to be an adult. I like being an aunt. I adore my nieces. But I don't want kids. I cherish being alone."

—*Felicia*

"Whoever I marry will have to wait till I'm ready to have kids. We'd have to be clear about it. I'd consider freezing my eggs, then marrying and having the kid in my late thirties or early forties." —*Katy*

"At twenty-eight I have a fertility fear. I'm thinking about freezing my eggs. It seems like a smart, businesslike decision." —*Martha*

"I'm obsessed with kids. I froze my eggs. I gave myself the injections, and out of twelve eggs, nine were good. My father said, 'It's like your insurance policy.' If I have to go it alone, I will." —*Jennifer*

o o o o

In your twenties you're testing your adventurous spirit in a thousand ways: building a career, dating, developing several circles of female and male friends, traveling, and generally leading a full-to-the-brim life; then one day you look around and you're closing in on thirty; then you're in your midthirties or late thirties. Where did the time go?

Maybe a first marriage or long-term relationship went south, and now you're on your own. Or perhaps you *could* have settled into a relationship just for the sake of being married and having a child—but you just did not want to. Maybe you didn't meet the right man until you were well into your thirties, or maybe you haven't yet met him or her yet. You probably never intended to push the fertility envelope, but life throws a lot of curve balls at *everyone*.

I like to see assertive Alphas calling the shots. What I *don't* like to see is adventurous, career-oriented women panicking when they hear the ominous ticking of their biological clocks. Once you're in your thirties, you may find yourself dating "with a gun to your head." It's hard to know how much time you can afford to give to someone you meet and like, but feel unsure about.

Here the intersection between technology and culture offers options, like egg retrieval, donor eggs, sperm donations, IVF, or surrogacy, for women who might not fall in love and marry in time to become pregnant. Alpha and Beta women alike take risks with fertility, but for different reasons: an Alpha, busy with work and her packed personal life, feels on some level that she has no limits. She may feel that she's in control, that she can outmaneuver her biological clock. As time passes, while the Alpha focuses on making huge career advances, her more relationship-oriented Beta friend or sister may be in a relationship but afraid to confront her ambivalent partner about what she wants.

For all of these reasons, fertility technology has become increasingly important. There's been a great deal of controversy about the women who choose to use it or even consider it. To some, the whole subject is an opportunity to chastise women for waiting too long. It's women's penalty for not being feminine enough and for delaying marriage. In other words, infertility is punishment for being too independent and self-sustaining. Christine Rosen, in the *Wall Street Journal*, opined that "egg freezing offers yet another technique of control in the process of having children. The more control we have, the more we expect the end result—the child—to turn out the way we want it to, and the greater our disappointment when he does not."

The idea that women are cold and narcissistic in their pursuit of fertility is toxic. When Sarah Elizabeth Richards wrote in the *Wall Street Journal* that her own personal experience with egg freezing, between the ages of thirty-six and thirty-eight, "stopped the sadness that I was feeling at losing my chance to have the child I had dreamed about my entire life," she was called "self-absorbed and calculating," among other insults. Richards believes that women resist the idea of egg freezing because they fear being seen as belonging to the "pampered, entitled generation of have-it-all feminists."

Don't let this kind of judgmental nonsense stand in your way if you're considering this option. Go ahead and think out of the box; do your research and come to your own conclusions. Older marriage and motherhood is a huge trend that isn't going away: according to the Centers for Disease Control, birth rates have risen for all women ages thirty and older since 1990. The more education a woman has, the later she tends to marry and have children.

Many fertility doctors, like Alan Copperman, MD, director of the Division of Reproductive Endocrinology and Infertility at Mount

Sinai in New York City, predicts a day when "there will be genomic tests done of young women in their teens and twenties to know whether they are destined to be fertile into their fourth decade of life and beyond, or whether they will have reproductive issues and should consider electively freezing their eggs." In *Slate*, Sarah Elizabeth Richards reports that fertility doctors are seeing increasing numbers of new patients. "For this age group," she says, "egg freezing . . . is a tool to plan their futures. It's liberation from constraints of biology."

In the *Atlantic*, psychology researcher Jean Twenge investigated the "popularly held belief that women's fertility takes a nosedive at 35." Twenge raises the panic-button age from thirty-five to forty. She found that some of the statistics are so bogus as to be laughable: the source of data, quoted in the journal *Human Reproduction*, saying that one in three women, ages thirty-five to thirty-nine, will not be pregnant after a year of trying, turned out to be French birth records from 1670 to 1830! Incredible!

Twenge cites analysis by David B. Dunson of Duke University's Department of Statistical Science showing an age-related decline in female fertility, but not the *plunge* that the older studies had shown. Anne Steiner at the University of North Carolina School of Medicine, whom Twenge also quotes, said that her data about fertility does not show "huge drops until age 40."

But for now, doctors are cautious. The American Society for Reproductive Medicine has announced that egg freezing is no longer experimental, but the organization is still "not ready to endorse for widespread use . . . Success rates decline with maternal age." More work has to be done before egg retrieval is a sure thing. A promising new technique called vitrification—flash freezing—has helped make the procedure much more successful in young women in terms of egg survival.

Twenge also warns that the data is "imperfect" at this point. So as science advances into unknown territory, I advise my clients to stay informed. Don't live in a perfect-baby bubble. Technology is a double-edged sword: while it empowers you by offering options, it also can lull you into thinking anything is possible—forever. Some women are counting on technology to extend their possibilities indefinitely, or they're in denial about the facts of life. I have an unmarried client who, at forty-four, believes that she can still have a baby without artificial means. Well, maybe—but not very likely.

In a *New York Times* article, writer Amy Klein described the first time she spoke to a gynecologist about fertility. She was forty years old and had just gotten engaged. When she asked the doctor how long she should wait after stopping the pill before she should try to get pregnant, the doctor said, "I really don't think you have any time to waste."

The writer was very offended by the doctor's snide tone. But frankly, I don't think you should be taken aback by straight talk. Klein goes on to say that women should reject ageism; at the same time she herself had difficulties. She got pregnant twice and miscarried twice and next chose the route of in vitro fertilization.

Sarah Elizabeth Richards notes that increasing numbers of women—and younger women as well—are choosing the procedure. Just remember: timing is everything and women who want children, with or without marriage, need to keep their eye on the clock.

PLAN B

It makes sense that once you decide to take charge of your fertility, the perpetual knot of anxiety in your stomach may relax a little. Jennifer, thirty-seven, decided to freeze her eggs because she didn't want to be frozen out of motherhood. At the same time she felt "much less pressured" about dating because it "changed the dynamic." Dating while panicking about fertility isn't a good way to stay focused enough to search out a good life partner.

Jennifer was lucky in that she could afford the procedure (uncovered by her insurance), and that she didn't suffer unpleasant hormonal effects from the self-administered injections (other women have told me that they do). "Injecting myself was a lonely feeling, though," she admitted. "That was the worst part. I rented a lot of movies and took a lot of walks. But it was only for a couple of weeks."

My client Vicki, after much soul-searching, did the same. At thirty-seven, newly divorced and very anxious, she panicked when a male friend warned her that most guys in her age bracket were only looking for sex. "Don't say that!" she told him furiously. But really she'd lashed out at him for saying what she didn't want to hear. She was killing the messenger, because she didn't like the message. Her anger masked her fear that what he was saying might be true. And that's when she decided to get real.

She said, "I've always envisioned myself as a mother, but I see that maybe I won't be able to have children with a partner. Still, I don't want to give up being a parent."

Several months later Vicki embarked on three rounds of egg retrieval. Emotionally, this was a huge deal because she had to envision a new identity, in which she confronted a very different life from the one she'd imagined. Resetting one's trajectory requires resilience and flexibility, and I admire women gutsy enough to do it. Vicki hasn't given up on meeting someone to have a family with, and chances are good that she will, but now she has a backup plan.

You shouldn't make your entire life revolve around your biological clock, but you do need to watch the time. If a woman in her twenties and early thirties who has other things on her plate wants children, she should keep that thought on the back burner but remember it's there. In her late thirties, my client Rachel made an egg-retrieval plan B. It was sad for her to confront the possibility of going ahead alone. Giving up on a dream of love, partnership, and a traditional type of family is a huge loss.

Rachel takes a clearheaded view of what lies ahead: she knows she'll have to scale down her lifestyle and move from Manhattan to New Jersey to be closer to her family. Her life would be very different from that of a freewheeling single working woman—but she can envision it. "Maybe I don't have to be married," she says thoughtfully. Rachel is making a radical shift in the way she perceives herself.

A single mother's family or circle of friends usually takes center stage in this new phase of her life. A client of mine, a first-generation Hispanic woman from a traditional immigrant family, was afraid to tell her parents that she planned to do egg retrieval. The family had been anxiously introducing her to suitable men, all of whom she considered totally unsuitable—"they couldn't *be* any wronger!" she told me with a grimace—but she didn't want to hurt her parents' feelings. Then, when her sister egged her on, she nervously laid it out for them—and was happily astonished to the point of tears when both her mother and her father were completely supportive. They were proud of her success in their adopted country, and the last thing they wanted was for her to miss out on the life she had envisioned.

And then there are the "worried well"—who need to relax. My client Robin was extremely anxious about meeting someone in time to have a child. "You have time," I reassured her, wondering why she was so worried about fertility at the age of thirty-one. The widespread knowledge and availability of high-tech options can cast a pall on younger women. Another reason for anxiety: one by one Robin's friends are getting married and having children. She's the only single woman left among the people she knows. But the fact is, panicking isn't necessary and it won't help. At her age there's no objective reason to succumb to fertility angst. She's at the stage when she needs to be clear and realistic and focus on the partner she wants to find.

ANOTHER PLAN B

If you want a baby, trust me, you'll find a way. Some women break out of the box and adopt on their own. Being determined and assertive helps this process. In fact, adoption harnesses all of your Alpha qualities: you need to be a genius multitasker to deal with the challenges of single-parent adoption. Think through the process beforehand, and prepare to discuss your long-term financial situation with an adviser you trust. Be sure you can be solely responsible for a child, not only financially but emotionally.

If you're adopting on your own, you will need to be single-mindedly determined as you research appropriate adoptions and take on bureaucracy and/or lawyers. Be prepared to be evaluated, to wait, and to travel. The unpredictability and uncertainty of the search and the waiting time may be a mindblower for the Alpha woman who is so used to having control over her circumstances.

Although rising numbers of singles are adopting, it may still be somewhat more difficult for single people to adopt than it is for couples. Once you do return home with your child, you may find, as do many adoptive parents, the single-parent lifestyle to be quite daunting—yet not impossible.

If you have an uncommitted or wishy-washy partner, confront the possibility of losing that person and be clear that you may have to go it alone. This is probably terrifying, but it's better than fooling yourself into thinking the partner is in it for the long haul. At the next crisis (sickness or job loss), he may bail. Ask serious questions: find out where the two of you stand.

Lori, a high school teacher, adopted a child on her own—which in her wildest dreams she could never have imagined herself doing. She'd thought that maybe her boyfriend Glen would make a commitment, but ultimately she was disappointed. As the oldest of three sisters in a California family, Lori, with her tough, wry exterior was the family risk taker. At the same time her exterior masked low self-esteem; as the brainy daughter who stood up to a tyrannical father, she'd had the privilege of his favor but also the pain of his contempt and criticism whenever she seriously challenged him.

In her twenties she only knew that she had to put distance between herself and her father and establish a separate life. She had a stubborn streak (shades of her father!), and against her parents' wishes moved to New York while her sisters settled in the San Diego suburbs to raise families. She felt confident she was doing the right thing. In New York she got her teaching certificate and began a career, handling at-risk teenage girls whose lives were in constant danger of being shattered. "I learned so much from those girls," she said. "I had to be as tough as they were. They overcame so much adversity, and I respected that."

Glen, who was in his forties, lived directly across the hall in her Manhattan apartment building. They had an open-door policy, going back and forth to each other's apartments to share TV watching, meals, and beds. They were *almost* living together, to the point where Lori felt they had a committed relationship. She let things go like this for years, telling herself they both wanted the same thing: marriage and a child. (Even though she was stubborn and took risks, her low self-esteem undermined her by sneakily whispering that she shouldn't push too hard for her own needs.) When she hit her midthirties, Lori knew it was time to initiate a conversation about the future. But Glen balked; he was comfortable with the way things were. Now Lori had to seriously harness her Alpha: if Glen was not going to come through, she'd have to take matters into her hands.

She struggled to put aside the idea of a biological baby and embraced a mission to adopt a child from China. All on her own, which took great guts, she undertook the drawn-out adoption process, was ultimately approved, and traveled around the world for her daughter. In the company of several couples who were also going to adopt, she at first was acutely aware of her single status. She acted self-confident, even though she certainly wasn't feeling it. But by the time the group landed in China, they'd all bonded, and Lori was comfortably part of the community of adopters. She was consumed by a sense of mission and adventure. The moment she saw her daughter, she fell in love and returned with her to the United States in a state of ecstasy. As when she'd left California for New York, she experienced an overwhelming sense that she was doing the right thing for herself. She knew that her life was going to change forever—and for the better.

Back home, she was gratified when Glen fell in love with the little girl just as she had. "I put my rose-colored glasses back on," she says wryly. They cooked and ate meals together and shared child care, shopping, and other tasks. They looked like a family, acted like one, and certainly they *almost* were. But when Lori broke the taboo on talking about whether their commitment was long-term, Glen became spooked. He opted not to marry and become a full-time, committed husband and father. And he was not willing to take part in supporting "their" child.

Lori knew she had to take the initiative to mend her relationship with her father. To her amazement, when she told him that she'd adopted a child, he was thrilled and insisted on coming to New York to meet her. When he visited, he told Lori that he wanted to help her out financially. They even discussed her moving back to the West Coast.

Looking back, Lori sees her mistakes. She'd let things go on with Glen because she'd been afraid to push for her goals. Ultimately, she'd made things too easy for him. He liked the status quo: closeness, company, and convenience without commitment. He enjoyed the child without having to take responsibility. Devastated, but finally dumping the rose-colored glasses, Lori decided she needed more than his fickle support and made a final, agonizing break, then left Manhattan for California. There, she bought a small suburban house for herself and her daughter, near her two sisters, and got a teaching job. She never looked back. (PS: Her daughter has developed into the bossiest eleven-year-old on the block!)

DATING IN UNCERTAIN TIMES

This strange thing has happened to a number of my clients: just as they get serious about finding a relationship, guys their age suddenly get scarce. What is going on? Aside from the fact that many men in their thirties are not ready for commitment (see: Bachelors!), others may be gun-shy because they don't want to be pressured into marriage. Even if a man would actually prefer a woman his own age, he's likely to shy away because he knows he may have to make a commitment before he's ready.

I encourage women over thirty-five to consider dating divorced (youthful) men in their late forties and early fifties. Having worked with many "older" men, I have noted a willingness to have another child with a younger, independent woman. In fact, a man may look forward to the possibility of having another child and, as one guy put it, "starting over and doing better the second time around."

Other uncertainties spring up: a year or so after her divorce a client in her early forties with two children decided that she was ready for a new relationship. At the same time, her priority was to protect her children from any further disruption. She went out a few times with a man she met on Match, but told him that if they were going to have a sexual relationship, they'd have to both agree to go off the dating websites and not date other people. It had to be exclusive, she explained: as a mother with responsibilities, casual sex was not for her anymore. He was agreeable, and she took her profile down. But when she checked to see whether he'd done the same, she found that his was still up.

She confronted him, and he pooh-poohed it. "I'm not sleeping with anyone. I'm just dating," he explained. She suspected he was annoyed at being nudged, which made her skeptical about him, but she gave him another chance, and after that, a couple more. She wanted to give him the benefit of the doubt, but he was obviously not ready to be exclusive. If your Beta gets the better of you, you may give a man too many chances. For a divorced mom, one round will do; it's enough to show that the two of you don't want the same things. Go the Alpha route: one round, and no more.

THIRD TIME'S THE CHARM?

There is a great deal of disagreement about just how high the divorce rate is for second and third marriages, but suffice to say that you certainly want to get it right when you try again. Blended families, complete with exes and children of different ages with different needs, are complicated, so it's even more important to get a grip on your personality and relationship patterns.

Tessa, forty-three, who tested high Alpha/high Beta on the spectrum, tends to be attracted to men who are disproportionately passive and lacking in self-confidence (the classic "nine" personality). In her marriage she was the enabler, and in her next relationship she repeated the unhealthy pattern. By this time, unless she understands why she makes her choices and how she can change, she is pretty much fated to be an Alpha enabler.

Tessa recently decided to take a time-out from relationships to focus on therapy and her nine-year-old daughter. She knows she can't afford to make yet another mistake. "In the past I've fallen in love with dreamers," she ruefully admits. "I'm not attracted to wildly successful men."

Tessa has avoided the trap of pairing up with a fellow Alpha, only to fall into the trap of the Omega. Her marriage to Kevin started out blissfully. "We were on level ground," she says. "It was romantic. We were young, in New York, and broke. We could live on twenty dollars a week, and be happy." Trouble started when Tessa, a media executive, began making money. "Money made things easier," she says. "But I kept waiting for him to catch up to me." Kevin dreamed of being an entrepreneur and had lots of ideas, but could never quite finish a business plan. As a computer whiz, he dreamed of all kinds of apps but didn't have the patience and persistence to do any of the real work.

Meanwhile, Tessa continued to make her way up, up, up the career ladder. She laughs as she recounts the words of one interviewer: "I've never witnessed such unconflicted ambition before!" Tessa adds, "I was confident at work. I knew why I was in charge and I knew my goals. I was willing to go out on a limb and I was undaunted by failure."

Her relationship with Kevin started to unravel as her success spiked. She tried to manage him as she managed her huge and growing staff. Arguments ensued, which landed them in my office. In couple's therapy, Kevin acknowledged their differences: "The core part of my initial attraction to Tessa was that she knew where she was going, and she knew how to get there. I had a different approach. I knew where I wanted to go, but I wanted to take a less direct way to get there."

"I thought we were both going places," Tessa says now. "I had a hand in a lot of start-ups. My work took us back and forth across the country, and to Europe. I always thought we'd live these wildly creative lives together. Two rock stars in orbit." Then their daughter,

Alyssa, was born, which, as children do, complicated their lives even more. When Alyssa was six months old, Tessa admitted to herself that something had gone very wrong. "I knew Kevin was unhappy," she says. "But I was so busy I wasn't paying attention to *how* unhappy he was."

Tessa's successes had taken over their lives; feeling dwarfed by her, Kevin had given up on building something of his own. Tessa was shocked to realize he no longer shared her dreams and that he'd fallen out of love with her and their life together. As an Alpha she always assumed that he wanted what she wanted. This overconfidence and self-centeredness skewed her perceptions and behavior. As Kevin thought of himself as an add-on, Tessa thought of Kevin as an extension of herself.

At this juncture in therapy, I pushed for discussions and an exploration of their expectations of each other. Being unrealistic about a partner can be one of the most insidious relationship busters. Usually, it's linked to blocked avenues of communication; after some candid discussion, Tessa was able to realize that Kevin wanted quite a different life from the one she'd envisioned—and she was shocked. Shocked.

In a grand gesture, she handed his life back to him: "Go and be the man you want to be," she said, concealing her pain and disappointment with a brave show of generosity.

Tessa should not have been as shocked as she was—which she can now admit. At the time of the divorce, she was thirty-four. Ten years later, as she looks back at those revelatory and terrifying moments, she says, with an ironic gesture, "I made a perfect marriage *after* my divorce. Kevin and I are awesome co-parents. It's unconventional, but we honestly do share parenting very well. We are a different kind of family. We both keep Alyssa's interests front and center."

But she admits, "I still run the family. I'm the primary parent." She sighs. "It's annoying." It was no longer what Tessa wanted, but she didn't see how to change the dynamic that continued even after the divorce.

Once things settled into a routine, Tessa went on a dating website and met Mark. He was tall and handsome and charming. "I fell in love," she says. "And it really was for the first time in my life." But she repeated the pattern she'd followed with her husband. "I can see now exactly how it happened. I ran the show. He became overwhelmed by my life, and his life floundered. Every week I moved the checkers on the board, planning evening events, arranging sitters and play dates for Alyssa. I can do a billion things at once, but he didn't feel he had an anchor in our life."

During this time Tessa's mother died, leaving Tessa grief-stricken. As a "parentified" child, she'd been her mother's caretaker; as an adult, she had an ambivalent relationship with both parents. If you're ambivalent toward your parents, losing them may lead to prolonged grief that goes deeper than it does for people whose relationships are healthier. Unresolved issues, like disappointment, anger, resentment, and longing, complicate mourning and make it more difficult to let go. You realize you'll never have the good parent you wish you'd had, and it can be heartbreaking. Tessa felt helpless and mystified by her grief: especially unnerving for a woman accustomed to control and success.

"I had to lean hard on Mark," she admits. "It was a lot. I needed his help. We were living off my paycheck. He helped, with cooking and groceries, and he was great with Alyssa, but I think it was too much for him." Mark, accustomed to having Tessa take care of him, could not muster up the Beta qualities needed to support her struggle.

Then things went badly at work, and "I walked away," she says. Her next job was a step down. "I only like being the boss," she says. "I'm spectacularly bad at being a regular employee."

Without a basis of mutual support, Tessa and Mark split up. She saw it coming and prepared herself emotionally for the end. Afterward, she knew she had to apply her brains and energy to making some serious changes.

Thoughtfully, she says, "For years everyone said I was 'amazing.' I always knew I'd age out of amazing. The question is, 'What now?'"

A year has gone by since Tessa and Mark split up, and she is in no hurry to meet someone new. "I haven't been looking for a relationship," she says. "Alyssa is my first concern. I am picking up the pieces from my relationships and the loss of my parents. I am not sure I understand who I am anymore. My career is in flux, and I have lost some confidence and bluster. I realize that criticism is hard for me to hear. But you're either crushed by your experiences, or you learn from them. I've decided to learn."

With her strong Alpha, Tessa obliterates men as much as she enables. These partners become totally absorbed into her world—then feel compelled to leave to regain a sense of self. "I learned," she says, "that someone can be the closest person in the world to you and you may not know them at all." It's true, and it's humbling, but you don't have to leave it at that. You *can* get to know someone a whole lot better if you develop stronger communication and listening skills. In therapy, Tessa needs to embrace her Beta and pick up cues, make time to talk, intuit feelings. She should pay close attention to her observing ego so she is more aware of her tone of voice and word choice. "You have to really, really listen to criticism," she says. "And let it change you." And then Tessa needs to partner with a Beta man who can hold his own with her.

"Next time, I want to feel that I'm sharing a life with someone," she says. I place the emphasis on *sharing*: leading is one thing; dominating is another. Her native self-confidence, now leavened by life experience, will help Tessa move on. People do learn from their mistakes, and with her willpower and energy, Tessa has a good chance to find a better way next time around.

AN INCONVENIENT PREGNANCY

At thirty-nine, Cindy was hit simultaneously by three life-changing events: a job offer in another city, a relationship crisis, and, last but hardly least, a pregnancy. For a while, thinking they'd stay together, Cindy and Jake had stopped using birth control—but problems between them had persisted. She had been dying to accept the job offer in Boston (it was a big promotion), but Jake hadn't wanted to move. She'd felt as if she had to choose between her relationship and her career. By the time Cindy found she was pregnant, they'd decided to separate.

Terrified of losing Jake and the possibility that she'd be having the baby on her own, Cindy came to see me. As she shared her confusion and upset, she broke down in tears repeatedly, but gradually realized that in spite of everything she was excited about the pregnancy. By now Jake had moved across town, and she suspected that he'd already started to date. When she tried to discuss the pregnancy, he was vague about how he felt but left open the possibility that he'd have a relationship with the child. "Anything is possible," he said.

Now she began to focus on some crucial questions: Could/should she have the baby without Jake? Would he want to participate outside of marriage? Should she take the Boston job? How could she deal with all of this? Over the next month, she decided to have the baby and move to Boston. With renewed spunk and confidence, she faced a future she could never have foreseen even a short time before.

She started considering Jake's true intentions. What kind of father would he be? She panicked at the thought that he would be in and out of her life, creating havoc. As we talked it over, she realized that she should not count on him for support, financial or otherwise. She was on her own. The more she thought about the situation, the more she realized she would go it alone.

We decided that she would be wise to consult a lawyer, who told her that if she wanted to ensure that Jake could not prevent her from moving to Boston, she should *not* put him on the birth certificate, nor ask him for support of any kind. In this way, unless he aggressively pursued paternity, he would have no control over her life or any say in her decisions about the baby. If he wanted a relationship with their child, it would be her call—and it would depend on his interactions with her and the child. It seemed to me Cindy was discovering another, deeper layer of Alpha that many women find when they become mothers, which includes an ability to have control over her life and to protect her unborn child from an unstable and perilous family situation.

Cindy is now in Boston, awaiting the birth of her child. She and Jake are in contact, but he is showing little interest in participating in the birth. Fortunately, Cindy has a sister nearby who is excited about helping her transition to her new life. Cindy says she feels like a pioneer charting unknown territory, and while she doesn't deny that she's scared sometimes, overall she sees her impending motherhood in terms of a rebirth. And as a bit of a surprise to herself, even after everything she's been through, she is able to stay open to Jake eventually creating a different kind of paternal role in their new family.

A TIGER MOM BITES BACK

When I see successful Alpha women opt out of their careers to stay home with their children, I get nervous. It is often a sign of present or future trouble in the marriage. Carla, who had an upper management position at a large university, was married to Derek, an Alpha businessman. The couple met when they were in graduate school; as foreign students in a new country, they were both lonely and clung to each other. Soon after getting their degrees, they tried to get academic jobs, but nothing panned out. They married while Derek went on to get an MBA and Carla, a degree in public policy.

After their children were born, Carla elected to stay home with them. From being a career woman steadily advancing up the ranks at the office, she became an Alpha mom, running the household like a major corporation—every button buttoned and every hair on each of the three children firmly in place. She invested all of her ambition and energy into the children and the home. Everything was regimented and structured to a T. Her devotion to her family was her whole life.

Derek, whose career in finance had taken off, complained that she was too controlling; she created too much stress at home because her standards were too high, and she was constantly bossing him and the children around. He resented her demands and began to treat her disrespectfully; while she was still at work they'd been equals, he'd thought. But now they had a much more traditional marriage. Carla was indeed a perfectionist, a loving but demanding tiger mother, who insisted on music and language lessons, and much, much more, for the kids.

One day Derek dropped the bombshell: he had fallen in love with someone else. Carla was devastated and desperately focused her energies on turning herself into the deferential, adoring wife. She couldn't see that it was futile to hope he'd love her if she toned herself down into a mouse. To the contrary, the more deferential she became, the more he ran over her. He moved out of their house and in with his new girlfriend. Flattened by the loss of status as a married woman, Carla was unprepared to negotiate with him about joint custody of the children. ("Who am I if I am not Derek's wife?" she would ask.)

In the course of their ugly divorce, they fought nearly to the death. It seemed as if everyone was playing dirty, including their couples therapist, who knew all along that Derek was having an affair. When a couples therapist colludes with one partner in hiding an affair from the other, he is condoning the behavior and guilty of an ethical violation. Carla, who was in individual therapy with me, was devastated; it amounted to a double betrayal. I explained that the therapist's behavior was unethical and advised her to confront him. Difficult as that was for her, she did so—and when he accused her of being paranoid (!) she dropped out of couples therapy. Hurt and confused as she was then, things got a whole lot worse.

It seemed that every few minutes Carla got another nasty text about her being too controlling with the children. Derek accused her of trying to prevent him from seeing them by not deferring to his all-important schedule. He would say he'd get the kids at a certain time, then shoot off a text that he was canceling. He'd name another time, and tell her she had to comply. If he had a free half hour, he'd text and announce he was going to swing by. And text after text brought acrimony about money.

He humiliated her in public by showing up for school events with his girlfriend. She became almost phobic about the ping of her iPhone; it only signaled another jab. Finally he began to threaten to seek sole custody of the children. After months of groveling at his feet, she grew to hate him, but the hatred was mixed with fear so debilitating that it nearly paralyzed her. Three times a week in my office I picked Carla up from the floor and set her back on her feet. At first I didn't understand where so much fear was coming from; objectively she had no reason to fear that Derek could or would take the children. She was a warm, caring mother, and Derek had no grounds to accuse her of neglect. I told her, "Unless his lawyer found you living in a plastic trash bag on Fifth Avenue, there is no way he could take your children away."

Finally I realized that Carla was undergoing a series of losses so great that they distorted her view of herself. She felt powerless— formerly powerful at the office, now stigmatized as a discarded wife, invisible as a mother, unworthy as a person. These feelings of loss and diminished status could lead only to the ultimate loss: that of her children. She had an irrational fear that Derek would eventually win and get everything he wanted. "He is just bullying you," I assured her over and over.

The more powerless Carla felt, the more Derek seemed to *sense* that. He demanded that the children stay with him half the time and introduced them to Courtney, his girlfriend. By now the children had easily figured out that she was the girlfriend who had broken up their family. They hated her, but Derek insisted that they come to him even when he wasn't going to be home—leaving them with Courtney or a nanny. One time while they were staying with him, a child got sick at school and no one but Carla was available to pick the child up. The children were having a hard time with the transition to two households, and all three had sleeping problems. I reiterated to Carla that there was no way in the world that Derek was going to get custody.

Finally, Carla hit bottom, and pushed back. One day when he texted to announce that he was dropping by, she pulled the plug on his behavior and texted back, all caps: *NO. KEEP TO THE SCHEDULE.* He threw a temper tantrum, claiming that she was preventing him from seeing the children, but instead of caving, she reclaimed her power. When she and her daughter were invited to a bat mitzvah, Derek told her that he was attending—with Courtney. Carla called the mother and asked if Courtney had been invited. The mother assured her that Courtney had not been invited and she'd make sure Derek knew that.

"What chutzpah!" I said, when Carla reported this to me. "You hold your head up high and go to that party!" Pretty soon, with my support and her ability to harness her core emotional strength, Carla became less reactive. She held her ground, getting stronger every day as she did so. Doing what was in the best interests of her children called up all of Carla's latent Alpha, which had been buried beneath a landslide of losses and bullying on the part of her spouse. She finally got a good lawyer and a good financial planner—and fought like hell. She questioned a parenting plan that allowed him visitation rights when he wasn't at home. She resisted his plan to take back the family home once the kids were grown. She even stopped his harassment by text. Once she drew the line, she got her life back—and the lives of her children. It wasn't easy. After being so rejected and humiliated, she could have become spiteful, but she resisted the urge to retaliate and stuck to a parenting plan that was best for their children.

Carla has also tamed her tiger mother tendencies, realizing that in the aftermath of the divorce her kids needed her support more than her discipline. She's now begun to recognize that making her children and her home her whole life will not work in the long run. She has to get her own life back. Now she is slowly piecing it together: joining a yoga studio, arranging a tennis league, taking some courses; all of these things are good outlets for her energy and organizational skills. I encouraged her to go to a spa on occasional child-free weekends. This was daunting for her, but when she went and found support among a number of other divorced moms who were there licking their wounds, her eyes were opened to the reality that she was not alone.

During one session, when she heard the ping of a text coming from her purse, she smiled, remembering her phone phobia, when she never knew what new outrage Derek was going to spring on her. "I feel like I've been through a war," she said. "Now I can do anything!" As we work together, Carla presents herself with new challenges: "I want to be more confident. After what I've been through, I am always looking over my shoulder thinking other people are better, smarter, cleverer."

As she learns to apply her tiger-mom Alpha qualities outside her home, she will without a doubt develop into the confident, secure person she aspires to be in all areas of her life. Divorce, paradoxically, is not always the worst thing that can happen—not if you come out of it with deeper self-knowledge and an ability to manage your emotions in crisis situations.

SOMETIMES I *WILL* BREAK THE RULES

Strong women know when it's necessary to break the rules and go their own way. Tracy, forty-six, has that quality in spades. She has a knack for doing well in the kinds of work situations in which other people founder. She has worked for some of the most difficult top management in her business: hard-charging extreme Alpha women who ran tight ships but who always respected and leaned on Tracy for her advice, her smarts, and her talents. Early on, Tracy discovered she seemed to have the golden touch. With a gift for going her own way, she kept her independence and intellectual integrity, without giving in to the temptation of making alliances, gossiping, or listening to the complaints of other staff members, which earned her the trust of her bosses. Tracy knew how to take care of herself.

When she and Simon married they'd known each other for eight years. He seemed to admire her independent spirit, and she thought he was a fairly mellow guy, which she liked. After a while, though, he began to challenge her. He resented her independence: if she so much as said *I* instead of *we*, he'd object. He accused her of second-guessing him, usually assumed she was trying to diminish him, and was hypersensitive to slights and hurts. He wanted her to bend into a more traditional coupledom than she was comfortable with, even insisting that she let him lead her across the street—as if she couldn't manage to face traffic without help.

For her part, Tracy was very stubborn and treated her husband's complaints dismissively. She had little motivation to salvage her marriage and didn't work very hard at it. She was so turned off sexually she'd have to smoke pot to relax enough to have sex, submitting without any desire or any real joy. Marital therapy did not work: because there was so much animosity and not enough mutual respect, their power struggles led to impasses.

Soon after Tracy and Simon decided to separate, she met Doug at a party. They spent the evening together, discovered they both had unhappy marriages, sensed each other's unhappiness, and felt a strong connection. Afterward Doug texted her a surprisingly intimate message: "What makes you happy?"

She replied immediately: "We need to talk about that."

They got together for coffee and then for dinner. "We were so compatible," Tracy says. "We were two unhappy people, but I'm a very positive person. He was so miserable, and I became his closest confidante."

On the questionnaire, Tracy identified herself as a risk taker; at the same time, she answered affirmatively to the statement "I follow the rules," but added a caveat. "I *will* break the rules," she says, "when something is really important to me. I knew Doug was married right from the start, but I liked him a lot; he was funny and warm and loving, and I really needed that. He made me feel alive again."

From the start he told her he wouldn't disrupt his life with a divorce. He was a Beta guy, who placed a high value on his family, and Tracy respected that. "He's kind, mellow, and a tender lover," she says. "But he won't upset the apple cart. He's risk averse." After a year or so, she became uncomfortable with the status quo. "It isn't that I wanted to get married," she says. But she didn't like being the other woman. She felt that it was demeaning to herself and unfair to Doug's wife.

She also felt she was facilitating his marriage: keeping it afloat by ensuring that Doug was in a happier frame of mind. "I understood that he's not like me. He always plays by the rules. I can be confrontational, but he can't. I understood all that, but I got fed up."

She decided to tell him that she could no longer abide by the parameters of their relationship. Most important, she explained, was that he had to decide what he wanted to do. It would not work for her if she commanded him to leave his wife; he had to make the decision either way and take responsibility. "I wanted him to be decisive," she says. "He had to figure things out for himself. I'm an independent, decisive person, and I expect a lot from other people. I was losing respect for him as he dillydallied."

Tracy had the toughness to pull herself away and, admittedly, use sex as a carrot to force him to make a decision. Determined and clear-headed, she knew just how much they'd both miss the companionship and the hot sex that had become central to their lives. But she didn't want to continue as they were, and it was obvious she had to make a move for herself; if Doug came around, that would be great. If he didn't, she'd move on. It was painful, but she viewed it as a calculated risk.

But just as she decided to start dating again, Doug contacted her to say he'd separated from his wife and moved out. Tracy bided her time, not sure whether to trust that the marriage was in fact over.

It's been two years since Doug left his marriage. And Tracy has stayed firm in her desire not to marry. "I knew I didn't want to," she says. Now Doug comes to her house, and her twins like him, but she understands that his children will never be part of her life.

Tracy's life is full with work, children, friends, and family. Her job makes her financially independent, and the children have relationships with both parents. She has a part-time relationship that she enjoys on her own terms, without marriage and the complications of a blended family. "I have exactly what I want," she says.

Tracy feels that she married a guy who wasn't mellow enough for her. And while Doug is a real Beta, he carries around a great deal of guilt—and debt. Since he left his wife, out of guilt he has taken on debt to keep her happy. Tracy says, "I'd really resent that if we were married."

Tracy, who is high in both Alpha and Beta, is neither a control freak nor a caretaker. Her best partner is a noncontrolling Beta with an autonomous streak of his own, who understands and respects her fundamentally independent spirit. She doesn't get caught up in pleasing other people, and though she's a highly involved, caring mom, she will not take care of a man. She can be calculating and is tuned in to her own self-interest (witness her ability to pull out of the relationship with Doug; usually this does not make a married man change his circumstances). If a partner gets in the way of what she knows works for her, she will not tolerate it.

THE CHEATING HUSBAND

Callie is high in Beta and in the middle range of Alpha. She comes from a family of independent women who tend to become involved with untrustworthy Alpha men. "I suspected for a while that Jack was cheating," she says. "One day I put on my private eye hat and went through all his credit card receipts." Her hunch was right: Jack, an architect and design consultant, was having an affair with his assistant. Jack was a supercharming guy, with a gift for gab and a taste for drugs, alcohol, and a high-rolling lifestyle. (The type of man to have fun with—but not to count on!) Callie had started her business as a floral designer, but when the couple had their two children, she scaled back. She'd uneasily felt that she was tamping down her mile-wide independent streak, but believed she could put it on hold and take it back when she was ready.

Things didn't turn out quite that smoothly. Nowadays, when Callie listens to her seventeen-year-old daughter talk about her plans to have what she thinks of as a normal life, she gets nervous. Her daughter vows to marry a successful guy, have five sons, drive an SUV, and live in a big house in the suburbs. She doesn't want the turmoil and loss she grew up with; she longs for stability and security. Callie worries because she knows it's a mistake to build an entire identity—not to mention a financial base—around being a wife and mother.

After their children were born, Callie and Jack grew apart. She was focused on the kids, and he was increasingly out in the evenings after being at work all day. She found that having him around made her unhappy because she sensed he wanted to be somewhere else. "When I first found out about the affair," she says, "I felt as if I'd simply confirmed what I already knew. We never talked, and I'd gotten to the point where I didn't even like him." They came for counseling for a year and tried to work things out. "It took me that long," she says. "The heart is not so easily resolved. But when I decided it was over for me, I felt good. I actually felt liberated."

When the couple divorced, Jack had no intention of telling their two high school–age children why they'd split. Callie insisted that they be honest, and she told the kids that it was the affair that had broken them up. "I don't know if it was right or wrong to tell them. But I didn't want to carry his secret around for him. *I* was honest; he was *not*."

Soon after Jack married his assistant, their baby was born. "The marriage and the baby were so hard for me at first," Callie says. "I was angry and jealous. On some level I knew it was the point of no return. It made the end of our life together all so final." But she had to manage her feelings. "I spoke to the kids about the baby, and I was supportive of their positive feelings for her. I wanted to have that rapport with them. They really loved the baby, but they hadn't wanted me to know that because they were afraid I'd be hurt. I wanted them to know it was all right for them to love her."

Callie and the children moved to New Jersey. "I didn't want to stay in the house, because it was so sad there. It was where I'd made this life for the family and then this awful thing had happened. My friends thought I was being impulsive, but I knew I wanted to start over. It felt good to be in a whole different world." After the divorce Callie struggled with how she was going to be strong for her kids, how she was going to face each day without showing her sadness, and how she was going to help them heal—and also try to take care of herself.

The worst thing was facing the reality that she'd lost her job as wife. Not knowing her role anymore put her on shaky ground. She just kept her head down and plowed forward. She started up her business again but felt she had to keep it low-key, so she could focus on the kids. She had to put her interests behind theirs, even though their interests depended on her emotional and financial well-being. Fortunately, Jack stayed proactive during that time: he drove to New Jersey on his visitation weekends to pick up the kids, and he kept the support payments coming regularly. "Problems came up," she says. "Of course it wasn't just him. It takes two to tango. But he tangoed somewhat more than I."

What Callie didn't realize was that her own trajectory echoed that of her mother's. When Callie was a child growing up in South Carolina, her parents' marriage fell apart and her mother packed Callie and her sister into the car in the middle of the night and drove to Arizona. Callie grew up without a father, curious about what family felt like. Then she unconsciously followed in her mother's footsteps by marrying an unreliable man, being hurt and disappointed, and making an impulsive geographical move to get out and start a new life. ("It wasn't a solution for my pain," she admitted. "I found out things follow you wherever you go.") Sometimes patterns are handed down from one generation to the next—unfortunate legacies that can only be ended by self-knowledge and a desire for change.

Fortunately, Callie also received a happier legacy from her mother:

strength and autonomy. After her mother brought her daughters back to their hometown, she had to fight to reestablish herself in the face of small-town gossip that had her as a wicked divorcée. She had the determination and gusto to rebuild her life. "She was a strong Southern woman," Callie says. "We may speak softly, but we're steel magnolias." Her mother got her teacher certification, and went to work. She was always busy, so Callie and her sister took care of themselves. "I have an independent streak that's a mile wide," she says.

It wasn't until three years after her divorce that Callie started dating again. She met five men online. ("One was a cross-eyed optometrist," she notes. "That was weird!") Then she met Ted. Ted was the opposite of Jack, she says. And in fact, he is the definition of a solid Beta guy: "very mindful, patient, and emotionally articulate." Ted moved in with Callie and the kids, which turned out to be more difficult than she could have imagined.

Callie quickly realized she wasn't ready to live with a man again. She wanted her independence and recoiled from sharing her life. It was shattering to both of them, but she told him he had to move out. "It was strange," she says. "But after that I realized a lot of things. I saw that I could only be comfortable with intimacy if I knew I could maintain my autonomy. And I knew that someday I could do that with Ted. I don't feel a need to marry, because I'm committed to the relationship. Ted is really special. I have trust issues, of course. But we both understand that the other needs space and time, and we abide by what we both need."

Eventually, Callie sold the house in New Jersey, and she and her daughters moved back to Brooklyn. She is keenly aware of their need for stability. "My daughter may make different decisions than I did, but I want her to understand the importance of independence, self-reliance, and being able to create joy for yourself. Women need to know that they can fall back on themselves. More challenges are coming our way, but I now see my life in terms of abundance instead of scarcity. Right now I'm working on myself. I'm ready to pull out the stops in my business, and I'm getting more excited about it all the time. I think there's enough air in my life for me to keep expanding."

FACING FERTILITY ANGST

- Ignore the negative press about women who delay marriage and childbearing. Many people haven't acclimated to what feels like a brave new world of choices. Hence, the culture reflects a surfeit of anxiety and uncertainty. Remember: you're trying to make the right choice for *you*; this doesn't mean you're spoiled and selfish or trying to engineer motherhood.

- "I tell people all the time that I froze my eggs," a woman in her late thirties said. She feels relieved, because she's taken action about something that worried her. Usually, families end up feeling happy and reassured even if their first reaction was negative. If you tell a man you're dating, he may be very positive and supportive—mostly because it relieves the pressure on him. Telling men you date, or anyone else, is always entirely up to you.

- Skip solutions that may cause trouble down the road: one woman considered getting sperm from her sister's husband. Not a good idea—this would make your brother-in-law the father of your child. This is too close for comfort; we don't know the psychological consequences. Another woman wanted to use leftover sperm from her gay sister's anonymous donor. This would make her child the half sibling of her sister's kids. Since she wants to get married someday, the arrangement might make a partner more uncomfortable than if she'd gone to the sperm bank.

- Consider carefully before asking a friend to donate sperm. It might work out just fine, but it *will* be complicated. Make sure you're both on the same page about the role—financial, emotional, legal—that he will play.

- Remember: the time frame for having a baby is not as cut-and-dried as it once was. It isn't fatal to the cause if you're unmarried and in your thirties. Know your options and be realistic.

CHAPTER 9

FREQUENTLY ASKED QUESTIONS

WHEN I BEGAN WRITING about the new Alpha woman and her Beta partner, I soon found out that people had strong reactions—both positive and negative—not only to the terms, but also to the ideas. The questions posed by colleagues, clients, friends, and families were thought provoking and begged to be answered. Here are a few of the questions (and my responses):

Q: It's interesting to look at the Alpha and Beta personality types. But isn't it simplistic to label people? Aren't you pegging people, by making them one or the other?

> *A: I am totally against stereotyping or pigeonholing. Human beings are far more complex; every one of us is an amalgam of personality traits, and no one is one-dimensional. The Alpha/Beta spectrum is designed to show you how we are all a combination of many kinds of characteristics, with many of us leaning more in one direction than the other. If your Alpha and Beta scores are within 10 points of each*

other, you are a true hybrid, which suggests that you are a well-rounded individual with a good dose of both personality traits. Today, as women gain ground economically and politically, they are showing Alpha behavior that used to be considered male. The Alpha/Beta spectrum challenges traditional concepts of feminine and masculine behavior as outdated and irrelevant.

Q: *Is it better to be Alpha than Beta, or vice versa?*

A: *Another no. Both have major positive qualities, although extremes in either direction are problematic. Each personality type has different strengths and weaknesses. Alpha women may be overly controlling while Betas may be too passive. Our culture is at a point in which Alpha traits in women are more permissible—whether those women are climbing the career ladder or running the local soup kitchen. Alpha traits, like self-confidence and the willingness to take on challenges, also help women deal with difficult life events. We live in a tumultuous age, and women are rising to the occasion. And this is why the Beta male—the type of man who can be supportive and provide genuine partnership—has become so important.*

Q: *Can you change your ratio of Alpha to Beta?*

A: *Absolutely—personality is not static. A parent dies, and you become more self-reliant. A marriage dissolves, and you take on responsibilities you never thought you could. The list goes on: a job challenge, parenthood, illness. All of these life events, predictable or not, can bring out dormant or less-developed personality characteristics. A year or a month or a few years from now, you may respond differently to the statements on the personality questionnaire in chapter 2, and find that your ratio has changed significantly. So, yes, personality is flexible: you can grow to meet new challenges.*

Q: *Are Alpha women always career women?*

A: No. You might be the head of the PTA, a genius at connecting people and forging new social or political relationships, or a mom who organizes and runs her household like a general runs an army. There are a million occasions in which your Alpha may be activated! Alpha women can be leaders at home and in the community, as well as in the office.

Q: *Aren't Alpha women ruthless?*

A: Let's define ruthless. Ruthlessness is when someone—male or female—doesn't care about the consequences of his/her behavior. This is an extreme, negative Alpha quality, and it is highly undesirable. But not all Alphas are extreme, so not all Alphas are ruthless.

Q: *Alpha women go after what they want, right? That makes me think they're selfish and self-centered.*

A: Again, let's define the terms. Self-centered and selfish have pejorative meanings, so the wording of the question suggests that being self-focused is a bad quality. Because women are encouraged to think relationally, being selfish has negative connotations for them. But thinking about yourself and your goals and putting yourself first are important ways to take care of yourself. It's healthy to make decisions that are in your own best interest. Sometimes this comes at the expense of someone else. There is nothing wrong with this unless you are generally impervious to other people's needs.

Q: *Are Alphas narcissists?*

A: No. The Alpha personality is not equivalent to the narcissistic personality. In the vernacular, the word narcissist is commonly used to describe a very self-involved person. Clinically, it's a personality disorder in which an individual is incapable of empathy or even of seeing another point of view. The narcissist is grandiose and filled with bravado, while at her core she lacks self-confidence. A healthy Alpha is genuinely self-confident and does not need to project an inflated sense of self to the world.

Q: *Are today's Alpha women comfortable with their competitive spirit?*

A: *Often they're conflicted. Women are socialized not to be competitive. In the olden days when women were called catty, manipulative, and seen as being undermining of one another, that kind of behavior was actually indirect competitiveness. They couldn't compete openly because it was frowned on, so they found other outlets for that very natural tendency. There is nothing wrong with direct, open competition, and I think women will grow into it. A self-confident person doesn't need to undermine other people in order to get ahead. Once women feel that it's OK to overtly compete, they will be more comfortable with themselves and more open about their goals.*

Q: *How do Alpha women differ from Alpha men?*

A: *In general, women are socialized to be relationship oriented, so Alpha women tend to be more collaborative and more focused on bringing people together than Alpha men might be. As Hillary Clinton pointed out in a* New York Times *piece, "Leadership is a team sport." Alpha males tend to be more hierarchical, less consensual, and may create an openly competitive atmosphere. Speaking about her own sense of herself as a leader, one of the Alphas in this book put it this way: "I don't have to be the number-one boss lady; I can collaborate. I am cognizant and respectful of other people's skills." Alpha women and men may have different leadership styles, but as women are adapting to the competitive male work culture, men are adapting to the feminine managerial style.*

Q: *Look, women and men are biologically different. This has to mean that some personality differences are preordained, right?*

A: Sure, but that doesn't account for the cultural divide in terms of roles and personalities that we've seen until now. That masculine/feminine divide has reflected a power dynamic in couples and in the larger society that is based on men's economic dominance. Social roles are determined by social norms, not biology. In a more equal society, male and female behavior will become more similar.

Q: *I like your idea about Beta men. But I'm sexually attracted to Alphas. Are you saying I have to give up the idea of an exciting sex life if I want a good guy?*

A: Alpha guys can be very sexy! But so can Betas—and they make better lovers over the long haul and better partners, too. Isn't that ultimately what you want? Of course, you deserve to have great sex, but let's be real. Within a loving relationship with a man you trust and depend on, you can introduce variety and adventure. You are capable of making that happen.

Q: *Are you saying that women can and should have it all?*

A: May I rephrase the question? Can a woman have a satisfying career and a great family life? Yes, if she chooses the right partner. This is the most important decision you will make. If you pick someone who is not threatened by you, and will support your endeavors as much as you support his, you will be halfway there. There will be challenges, but you will be in a good position to go for broke.

Q: *Are Alpha women grown-up mean girls?*

A: Many people have asked me this question. I discussed it at length with a child psychologist colleague and threw it out to a focus group for comment. The consensus: mean girls hide their own insecurity by picking on other girls. The clinical term—relational aggression—describes a form of bullying that is designed to make the bully feel powerful and the bullied to feel powerless. A self-confident girl is not a bully; nor are mean girls blossoming Alphas—quite the opposite. Here is one woman's comment:

o   o   o   o

"You can be a queen bee in high school and that may be the best you ever do. This is true for some of the mean girls I knew in high school, and they are sort of pathetic. Others have surprised me by rising out of that stage and becoming mature adult women." —*Miranda*

o   o   o   o

Q: Are Beta women more feminine and Alpha women more masculine?

A: While Beta women demonstrate more traditionally feminine behavior than Alpha women and Alpha women demonstrate more traditionally masculine behavior, the gender line has become blurred. As a therapist in New York specializing in relationships, I began seeing more gender-neutral behavior in both my male and female clients over the last decade. I was fascinated by the shift and astounded by the new ways that relationships were unfolding in front of my eyes. These developments became the inspiration for this book.

o   o   o   o

Some women talk about so-called masculine and feminine traits:

"I am a high Alpha/high Beta. Even though I'm a feminist, I want some traditional things. I like to cook; that's a huge pleasure for me. If a guy will clean the bathroom, I'll do almost anything else." —*Melissa*

"I don't cook and I don't do traditional womanly things. I think my boyfriend was surprised and uneasy about that. It's been a big adjustment for us." —*Aimee*

"As an Alpha, I love to take charge and organize things. If he moves the car, I'm happy to get the bookshelves in order and plan our next vacation." —*Cara*

"As a woman, I've been called selfish. It hurt at first. But any time you prioritize your own life, people call you that. People say I'm intimidating to men. I think it's true. I've been called manipulative because I love to organize people— but I call myself a facilitator." —*Jill*

○ ○ ○ ○

Q: *As a high Alpha/high Beta, I love competitive sports as well as babies and cooking. Am I too retro?*

> A: *You are a complex, contemporary woman. Go for what you love to do; don't worry about shoulds or shouldn'ts. But do insist that your boyfriend/partner/husband contribute his fair share of the housework.*

Q: *If Alpha women are so straightforward and focused, why do they end up in bad relationships?*

> A: *Alpha women face several stumbling blocks in relationships. Some may think that the perfect matchup is the Alpha male. They couldn't be more mistaken! Since Alpha men have to be top dog, the relationship usually ends up in a huge power struggle. A supercompetent, problem-solving Alpha woman may choose an Omega male who needs a strong woman to organize his life and make all the decisions. This is a big mistake: caretaking a loser will bring you down. Don't go there!*

Q: *Do Alpha women engage in casual sex more than Beta women?*

> A: *Both Alpha and Beta women engage in casual sex as a way of enjoying their sexual drive while they focus on their career and personal*

goals. Beta women might look for a partner sooner than an Alpha. I worry about women who participate in casual sex to be cool and solicit approval from peers. Casual sex is fun for some and not for others. If you know you can't handle it, opt out. Don't ever do anything sexual that you don't want to do.

Q: *Aren't Alpha women strident feminists?*

A: *Now that's a blast from the past! To this day, strident is a loaded, negative term that raises everyone's hackles. What's wrong with being strong willed and assertive about women's rights and equality? Aren't we all in favor of those things?*

Q: *If you want a career and a family, when should you start looking for a partner?*

A: *There is no one-size-fits-all formula. More women are choosing to marry later, but you don't want to wait so long that you run out the biological clock. Marrying earlier means you need a partner who hasn't peaked and will grow up with you. There are lots of choices; you will find your own rhythm.*

Q: *I make more money than my husband. I can tell that his pride is hurt by this reversal of roles. What can I do to assuage his ego?*

A: *Beware of the desire to do more child care and housework to make up for taking the male role as the major breadwinner. Ultimately, you'll wind up exhausted and the problem still won't be solved. Talk to your husband about how you can share responsibility and divide the chores. His sweat equity as an active participant in the household should strengthen his role and boost his self-esteem. Remember: being successful is nothing to apologize for. Take pride in your contribution to the family's solidity and financial well-being.*

Q: Should Alpha women tone down their Alpha?

> **A: Some Alpha women need to step back and observe themselves. On the one hand there is nothing appealing—in male or female behavior—about being dogmatic and controlling. On the other hand you never hear of domineering men being called bossy. Being a bossy chick is not a glaring flaw—within limits. You might even say that bossy is back!**

Q: What do men need to do to adapt to the new social reality of empowered Alpha women?

> **A: Our old male-dominated society is giving way to a culture of partnership and collaboration. Men need to develop a new masculine ideal: that of being a great father, a great husband, and a great friend. How sexy is that?**

Afterword

A NUMBER OF PEOPLE asked how I went about developing the Alpha/ Beta questionnaire. Since enough inquiring minds wanted to know, here's how it happened: Once I identified the personality continuum and its potential for helping to develop healthy partnerships, I decided to create a tool people could use to understand themselves and recognize personal relationship patterns. First, I listed all of the Alpha and Beta attributes on the spectrum, from most positive to most negative. For instance, for Alpha, the questions ranged from "leader" (positive) to "domineering" (negative); for Beta, the questions ranged from "supportive" (positive) to "self-critical" (negative).

Then I considered how to translate behaviors into simple statements, to which people could answer, "Yes, that is me," or "No, that is not me." I tested the questionnaire on clients, focus group participants, and friends. Since it was important that the questions accurately reflect the relationship styles, I interviewed the participants at length in order to make sure that their scores matched up with their personalities and relationship histories. I modified many of the questions several times to get at the essence of the attributes that make up the Alpha and Beta personalities.

The questionnaire has an equal number of Alpha and Beta questions, which reflect the *degree* of Alpha or Beta. Since everyone has a combination of qualities, I needed to see the pattern or predominance of one set of attributes in relationship to the other. My goal was to make it possible for any woman or man to learn where their tendencies lie and identify their strengths and weaknesses.

There are many ways to use the questionnaire. Study your score; ask someone else to score you; throw a party in which you share and interpret your scores. Give it to your boyfriend/husband/lover, and see where there is a fit! This quiz is constructed to give you information about yourself and to help you grow.

High Alpha: 50 percent–100 percent
Mid Alpha: 25 percent–50 percent
Low Alpha: 1 percent–25 percent

High Beta: 50 percent–100 percent
Mid Beta: 25 percent–50 percent
Low Beta: 1 percent–25 percent

As a general rule: the closer your Alpha and Beta scores, the more of a hybrid you are, either at the high, mid, or low end of the spectrum. The further apart your scores are, the more pronounced one personality style is over the other.

REAL PEOPLE'S SCORES

A score of over 50 percent in both is a true hybrid. Let's analyze

Tracy's score (you'll read about her in chapter 8): Tracy had 70 percent Alpha and 54 percent Beta. This puts her in the high Alpha/high Beta section of the graph, meaning that she is a true hybrid: strong in both. Tracy is an independent, decisive woman, who is supportive and caring in a relationship. However, because her Alpha score is almost 20 percent higher than her Beta, she may sometimes be overbearing.

A high Beta/mid Alpha is a common score. Let's look at Amy (her story appears in chapter 6): Amy came in at 76 percent Beta and 40 percent Alpha. Amy has strong Beta tendencies (caring, dependable, thoughtful, and a little conflict avoidant); however, she has enough Alpha to stand up to a strong Alpha partner (and that is just the kind of man she ended up marrying).

References

CHAPTER 1: LOVING YOUR ALPHA

The Hamilton Project, "The Marriage Gap: The Impact of Economic and Technological Change on Marriage Rates, 2012."

Coontz, Stephanie (citing Leslie McCall, PhD), "The Disestablishment of Marriage," *New York Times*, 2013.

Council on Contemporary Families, 2010. "Myths About College-Educated Women and Marriage."

Coontz, Stephanie, "The Disestablishment of Marriage," *New York Times*, 2013. "With every year a woman delays marriage, up to her early thirties, her chance of divorce decreases, and it does not rise again thereafter."

Bertrand, Marianne, Emir Kamenica, and Jessica Pan, Booth School of Business at the University of Chicago, 2013.

Pew Research, "Women Make Significant Gains in the Workplace and Educational Attainment but Lag in Pay," 2013.

Luscombe, Belinda, *Time*, 2010. "Workplace Salaries: At Last, Women on Top."

National Committee on Pay Equity, 2007.

Pew Research, "The Decline of Marriage and the Rise of New Families," 2010.

CHAPTER 2: THE ALPHA/BETA SPECTRUM

Hyde, Janet Shibley, PhD, "The Gender Similarities Hypothesis," 2005. "A person's gender has *little or no* impact on most psychological traits, including aggression and passivity."

CHAPTER 3: SEX AND THE ALPHA WOMAN

Carothers, Bobbi, and Harry Reis, "The Tangle of the Sexes," *New York Times*, 2013.

Lavner, Justin A., Benjamin R. Karney, and Thomas N. Bradbury, *Journal of Family Psychology*, 2011.

CHAPTER 5: THE ALPHA AND BETA OF DATING

Experian Hitwise (Internet tracking firm), 2011.

CHAPTER 6: BECOMING A COUPLE

Pew Research, "Majority of Never-Married Adults Want to Wed," 2013.

Blakeslee, Sandra, "How One Woman Changed the Way We Think about Divorce," *Slate*, 2012.

Coontz, Stephanie, "The Disestablishment of Marriage," *New York Times*, 2013.

Martin, Steven P., PhD, University of Maryland, Russell Sage Foundation working paper.

National Center for Health Statistics, cited in Jay, Meg, PhD, *New York Times*, 2013.

Cherlin, Andrew, PhD, "In the Season of Marriage, a Question. Why Bother?" *New York Times*, 2013.

Coontz, Stephanie, "The Disestablishment of Marriage," *New York Times*, 2013.

US Census Bureau, 2012. The rate of cohabitation has risen from 450,000 couples in 1960 to 7.5 million in 2012.

Coontz, Stephanie, *New York Times*, 2013.

Cook, Lynn Prince, Council on Contemporary Families, University of Illinois at Chicago.

Cherlin, Andrew, PhD, "In the Season of Marriage, a Question. Why Bother?" *New York Times*, 2013.

Jay, Meg, PhD, *New York Times*, 2013. Couples who live together operate on the principle of "sliding, not deciding."

CHAPTER 7: AFFAIRS: PERFECT STORMS

Mark, Kristen P., Erick, Janssen, and Robin R. Milhausen, Indiana University, 2011.

Daily Mail, United Kingdom, 2013.

Hyde, Janet Shibley, and Jennifer L. Petersen, University of Wisconsin, 2010.

Center for Sexual Medicine at Sheppard Pratt, cited in "Unexcited? There May Be a Pill for That," *New York Times*, 2013.

Ourtime.com, 2012

Wall Street Journal, 2012.

CHAPTER 8: DIVORCING, DATING, SURVIVING, THRIVING

American Baby, 2013.

Bibliography

Bell, Leslie C., *Hard to Get: Twenty-Something Women and the Paradox of Sexual Freedom,* Berkeley and Los Angeles, California: University of California Press, 2013.

Coontz, Stephanie, *A Strange Stirring: The Feminine Mystique and American Women at the Dawn of the 1960s,* New York: Basic Books, 2011.

Fine, Cordelia, *Delusions of Gender,* New York: W.W. Norton and Company, 2010.

Gerson, Kathleen, *The Unfinished Revolution,* New York: Oxford University Press, 2011.

Rosin, Hanna, *The End of Men*, New York: Riverhead Books, 2011.

Sandberg, Sheryl, *Lean In: Women, Work, and the Will to Lead*, New York: Alfred A. Knopf, 2013.

Acknowledgments

FOR ABOUT TEN YEARS I thought about writing a proposal for a book about the new social world, focusing on the fascinating digital impact on the dating scene. As I wrote about that, I also added a few chapters on the Alpha personality and the new relationship dynamics I was seeing in my practice. As my early proposal developed, it was Susan Schneider, my coauthor, who kept saying, "The most interesting material here is the new Alpha woman and her relationship problems." Being headstrong, I disagreed.

At the same time, Ben Wolin, my son-in-law, who runs a media company, read an early draft. His first comment was, "Everyone knows the stuff about social media and texting. It is not that new." Ben convinced me that changes in gender-role behavior and their impact on relationships were the most interesting part of the proposal and should be the focus.

So, with Ben's help, I realized that Susan was right all along. Thank you, Susan and Ben, for putting me on the right path, a path that I actually had been on all the time without realizing it.

I am extremely fortunate to have a large active practice with some of the most interesting adults in New York City. These amazing women and men comprise the center of this book. They allowed me into their most private thoughts, sharing with me their frustrations, disappointments, and anxieties. They inspired and challenged me to come up with new ways of thinking. When the book was in its last stages of writing, I shared with them the stories that were created around their lives for their approval or retraction. Not knowing what to expect, I held my breath. Within days, I got a green light from everyone. I deeply thank all of you; you know who you are.

Among the first round of active supporters was one of my oldest and dearest friends, Jean Marzollo. She was one of our most helpful critics, and even more important, introduced us to her agents, Molly Friedrich and Lucy Carson at the Friedrich Agency. With these super-smart professionals on the project, we went through many exhausting versions of the proposal, aided by more members of the Friedrich staff of Alpha, Beta, and hybrid ladies, who helped refine the questionnaire. When we met Rachel Kahan, our editor at William Morrow, we knew we were lucky to have a brilliant editor with attitude.

My sister, Lynda Treger, and my close friends, Christy Guzzetta, Jodi Sayler, Susan Strang, Marcy and Peter Schuck, Joe DeLorenzo, and Barbara Kass, offered all kinds of encouragement throughout the project. Dr. Renee Epstein and Dr. Ellen Margolin, my close colleagues, rode the roller coaster with me every other Wednesday, and my new friends, Tina Weinstock, Barbara Solomon, Helene Grossman, and Gary Steinkolh, were wonderful in their feedback as we all anguished over the title. Loren Brill, a friend and young entrepreneur in the food industry, was enormously helpful in pulling together one of our best focus groups. I want to thank Dr. Cristina Matera, a fertility expert, who generously gave her time to critique our fertility data for accuracy.

Susan and I would like to thank the many other women whom we interviewed and who generously took the questionnaire. I am listing only a few: Kaylee Boalt, Stephanie Dolgoff, Tamara Hamdan, Cheyenne Huang, Shavonne Johnson, Karen Mason, Stacy Morrison, Sharon Richter, Heather Sipan, Maureen Stutzman, Veralyn Williams, Martha Watson, and Jenna Zimmerman.

All along, my family has been my sanctuary of support. Bob, my husband, who has been my partner forever, routinely jokes at dinner parties that now he's going to write a book called *Living with Alpha*. An architect, he designed the beautiful graph that is featured in the second chapter. Thank you, Bob, for your sense of humor and wisdom throughout.

I thank my son, Justin, a neurobiologist, for explaining how social norms are often erroneously explained by theories of natural selection and adaptation. I thank my daughter, Jennifer, a physician, and my daughter-in-law, Nancy, a veterinarian, for sharing with me the opportunities and challenges of being contemporary professional women with children. Women like them are the real heroes of gender equality.

—Sonya Rhodes, PhD

My daughter, India Schneider-Crease, a graduate student at Duke University in evolutionary anthropology and a fabulous young Alpha woman, offered us many priceless ironic remarks about the similarities between human primates and all the rest of the primates in their search for mates. She also pulled together a focus group of fellow graduate students to discuss the dizzying subtleties of online dating. Thanks to India, Chris Krupenye, Emily Boehm, Tessa Nin, and many more for their help. I also want to thank Martine Aerts-Niddam and Grace Bennett for their insights on the questionnaire. Finally, I want to thank William Koggan for his insights on gender and for coming up with the concept of scoring the questionnaire. My math fell short, and he kindly applied himself. Thank you, Wil.

—Susan Schneider

BOOKS BY SONYA RHODES

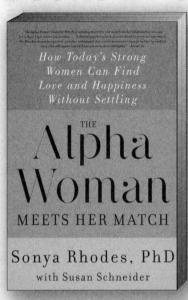

THE ALPHA WOMAN MEETS HER MATCH
How Today's Strong Women Can Find Love and Happiness Without Settling

Available in Paperback and eBook

In the twenty-first century, women are outpacing men in education and career advancement. Yet successful women are constantly being told that their professional achievements might doom their chances of marriage and family. Dr. Rhodes shares her secrets to helping women triumph in love by finding men who will appreciate and complement their strengths. Challenging gender stereotypes associated with the terms "Alpha" and "Beta," she advises the Alpha woman to look past the overly competitive, domineering Alpha male for a man who is not threatened by her strengths but is communicative, responsible, and collaborative. Just as Alpha women aren't demanding bitches, Beta men aren't passive wimps.

SECOND HONEYMOON
The Pioneering Guide for Reviving the Mid-Life Marriage

Available in Paperback

At mid-life, everything changes in most marriages. As the "family" focus shifts back to a "couples" focus, serious questions arise for each partner: *Who am I now? Who are you? Who are we together?* These questions go to the heart of a relationship, and the answers can often lead to conflict and, ultimately, divorce. Even the best relationships can founder as children grow up and leave home. More subtle and dramatic still are the profoundly different personal changes men and women undergo at mid-life. But as this wise, compassionate, and groundbreaking book shows, mid-life can also be a time for couples to examine and reinvent their relationships, renew their marital contract—and make a different kind of commitment to each other. *Second Honeymoon* explores the impact of mid-life on couples and the specific issues partners face.